The archaeological record consists of 'dead' finds, remnants of human culture. The archaeologist relies on them to understand how past societies were organized and how they functioned. This book, by the distinguished Czech scholar Evžen Neustupný, considers the archaeological method, the way in which archaeologists translate mute objects into descriptions of a living past. The method involves a series of steps: an analysis of the archaeological record; a synthesis of the finds to generate formal archaeological structure; and the use of models derived from descriptions of observed human activity to explain these structures. Without models, archaeologists would have no way of interpreting their finds. The author also considers the relevance of archaeology of such concepts as induction and deduction, empirical research and theory.

T0382636

Archaeological method

Archaeological method

EVŽEN NEUSTUPNÝ
Czechoslovak Academy of Sciences

CAMBRIDGE
UNIVERSITY PRESS

CAMBRIDGE UNIVERSITY PRESS
Cambridge, New York, Melbourne, Madrid, Cape Town, Singapore, São Paulo, Delhi

Cambridge University Press
The Edinburgh Building, Cambridge CB2 8RU, UK

Published in the United States of America by Cambridge University Press, New York

www.cambridge.org
Information on this title: www.cambridge.org/9780521115889

First published 1993
This digitally printed version 2009

A catalogue record for this publication is available from the British Library

Library of Congress Cataloguing in Publication data
Neustupný, Evžen.
Archaeological method / Evžen Neustupný.
    p   cm.
Includes bibliographical references.
ISBN 0 521 38076 6
1. Archaeology – Methodology.   I. Title.
CC75.N47   1993
930.1´ – dc20   92–1711–CIP

ISBN 978-0-521-38076-8 hardback
ISBN 978-0-521-11588-9 paperback

Contents

Tables

Preface

No progress in archaeology can be achieved by simply accumulating finds. The strategy of excavating in the hope that one day finds may begin to speak simply does not work. This is one of the reasons why so many archaeologists have recently become interested in theoretical and methodological problems. The main reason, however, is that the intellectual atmosphere in our modern society is changing under the influence of rapidly developing technology and social relations.

Changed attitudes have led to the need for a new paradigm in archaeology which has been built in the last twenty or thirty years. It should not be disquieting that results come slowly; I consider this to be a rather normal phenomenon as the principal building phase may still lie before us. Anyway, the angle from which the new generation entering archaeology at the beginning of the 1990s looks at the discipline has changed enormously. This is particularly conspicuous for someone who, like myself, has been brought up in times when the concepts of typology, diffusion and migrations represented the principal methodological and theoretical pillars of archaeology.

Despite the fact that most of my early papers dealt with specific archaeological problems quite acceptable within the traditional paradigms, my interest in methodology and theory began very early (E. Neustupný 1958). I formulated my methodological views as a whole for the first time in my dissertation in 1964 (published in Neustupný 1967, English summary p. 68) and later in my contribution to the 'Whither archaeology?' series in the British journal *Antiquity* (Neustupný 1971, written in 1968). Many of the concepts discussed in this book have been at least mentioned there (transformations, the use of modelling, the necessity of synthesizing archaeological structures, etc.). In later years I have mainly experimented with problems of analysis and synthesis of structures (Neustupný 1973a, 1978 etc.).

In 1983 I wrote a book on archaeological method whose contents and main ideas were similar to those presented here. The manuscript in Czech, destined for the general reader, has never seen the light of day because the publishers asked for changes that would turn it into a handbook on 'discovering archaeological treasures' (something which I have always disliked). A very short summary of the manuscript appeared later in the journal *Archeologické Rozhledy* (Neustupný 1986). I would almost have given up hope that my views would ever appear in book form were it not for Colin Renfrew's proposal that it should be published by Cambridge University Press. Although my principal theses have not changed, I have rewritten the book completely, leaving out whole chapters, rearranging others, and reacting to new ideas.

Living in isolation from the main centres of archaeological thinking in North America and Britain in the sixties I developed a different approach, some aspects of which have been described elsewhere (Neustupný 1991). I was influenced by the economic teaching of Karl Marx, mediating for me the earlier philosophers. G. W. F. Hegel may have left the greatest impact on my epistemology, mainly through his dialectics and logics. Systems theory and 'cybernetics' were equally inspiring in the formation of my early methodological views. And, of course, I have known the work of F. de Saussure since the fifties. This is certainly not a complete list of what I studied before approaching archaeological theory and method; what may appear striking, however, is the fact that this list does not contain any archaeological writings. This is not so much because of its brevity as because I did not find too much inspiration in this field. However, I should perhaps mention at least Montelius' chapters (1903) describing the typological method, still to be admired. Malmer's book (1962), representing the peak of the typological paradigm but nevertheless stimulating, arrived too late to influence me.

When I became aware of the so-called New Archaeology at

the end of the sixties, I immediately recognized its closeness to my own approach. There was no identity of views but I was convinced that something very important was being introduced into archaeology. In some respects I did not object to being influenced but, on the whole, I retained my original position. I admired Binford, David Clarke, Renfrew, Gardin and Schiffer (to name a few) for their ability to formulate new ideas and keep them within a system. I feel that Ian Hodder has enriched the concept of archaeology by putting stress on what I shall describe as the significance of facts. Some of the authors named in this paragraph might object to being included among the New Archaeologists, and in fact I also dislike the term. I believe, however, that the stream of archaeological thinking which leads from the sixties to the nineties cannot be divided into several paradigms.

The yearly increase in literature dealing with problems of archaeological theory and method is so great that it becomes difficult to keep abreast of all new contributions. At the same time almost all imaginable propositions have already been discussed and this makes it difficult for any author to be original on many points: almost all solutions have already been proposed. Originality is still feasible as far as a whole coherent system of ideas is concerned. This is, I believe, the sense in which this book may claim to be original. Its principal ideas will be summarized in the following paragraphs.

Various transformations turned once-living human culture into dead archaeological facts, reducing the information contained in those facts so drastically that the archaeological record consists of static, formal, object-orientated things with no observable function, meaning and significance. As a result, it is impossible to explain the archaeological record exclusively in its own terms: it is necessary to use models derived from contexts of human activity which are either directly observable in their live form or available in descriptions in some understandable (natural) language. The models, however, cannot be applied to raw data: it is essential to pass through the steps of analysis and synthesis. The latter produces (formal) archaeological structures which are compared to the models. In this way, explanation is achieved. The models should be used in several phases of the archaeological method, starting with description, which leads to the conception of the method as an endless iterative procedure asymptotically approximating the human past.

The volume consists of six chapters. Chapter 1 discusses the concept of archaeology and several other *preparatory concepts* which usually appear in pairs: archaeological means and objects, theory and method, induction and deduction, empirical and theoretical research, things and structures, and the role of mathematics in archaeology. The aim of this chapter is not a systematic treatment of the subject, but simply to explain the sense in which some of the general notions are used in the book.

Chapter 2 is concerned with two major prerequisites of the archaeological method: *archaeological records and paradigms*. Both must be present if the method is to operate. While the record is treated systematically (divided into artifacts, ecofacts and natural facts), the analysis of paradigms is orientated historically: the old 'traditional' paradigm is characterized in some detail.

Chapter 3 describes various kinds of processes which have *transformed* the past living culture into the archaeological record. Attention is paid to the exit transformation, to destruction and spatial replacement, as well as to the quantitative aspects of the process. The properties of the archaeological record resulting from transformations (lack of dynamics, loss of function, meaning and significance) become the starting point of the whole archaeological method, which can be conceived as a series of inverse transformations.

Chapter 4 discusses *analysis*, which is a decomposition (both physical during excavations and mental subsequently) of the record into various kinds of elements; the analysis results in description. This methodological step requires assumptions about the function, meaning and significance of the record which are necessarily 'imported' from models formed outside archaeology. At the same time, analysis produces elements which are devoid of function, meaning and significance and can be conceived as formal observable entities and qualities.

Chapter 5 describes a stage of the archaeological method which often remains undistinguished as an independent methodological procedure. The record decomposed in the phase of analysis must be synthesized again, this time on a higher level of abstraction. The products of *archaeological synthesis* are formal regularities in the record which are termed archaeological structures (traditional types or phases can serve as examples of structures in this sense).

Chapter 6 discusses how *archaeological structures*, which are dead formal entities, are given meaning in terms of a dynamic social and cultural system. The chief method used to accomplish this is modelling; rules for the generation and use of models are given. Models successfully compared to the archaeological structures generate a theory which can be used to start a new iteration of the whole of archaeological method.

As seen from the preceding paragraphs, my conception of the archaeological method does not include the technical tools (such as radiocarbon or geophysical prospecting) which are often identified with the theme. The purpose of this book is to demonstrate that archaeological methodology is a much broader issue; in spite of this, it differs from archaeological theory (cf. section 1.2).

The generality with which I am trying to cover the field has prevented me from discussing the existing literature at any substantial length. Attempting to refer to many (if not most) colleagues writing on the subject in recent years would not be realistic, bearing in mind the enormous quantity of literature in languages other than English. Since I do not claim originality in the case of most of the specific theses, I feel I can be excused for not including a more detailed bibliography.

In recent years, archaeology has become increasingly attractive to the general public. One of the reasons for this phenomenon is undoubtedly the fact that it has no elaborate terminology: the reading of reports on archaeological discoveries may not be always a thrilling experience but, in general, even fairly specialized papers are comprehensible to everybody. Our discipline is one of the last sciences which are still readable for a non-specialist. Only a few of the theoretical currents of the last twenty or thirty years deviated from this picture.

Should archaeology be proud of being understandable to everybody? Democratic science is certainly not expected to indulge in esoteric verbal rituals but I still believe that the present-day understandability of archaeology is more or less a consequence of its theoretical and methodological weakness. This is obvious from the fact that archaeological concepts rarely form chains in which the next link depends on the preceding one. However, the happy situation of being understood by everybody cannot go on for ever, because the reality which archaeology studies is not simple: complex relations cannot be described by means of simple terms. It is my conviction that archaeological terminology will become much more complicated in the near future and, as a result, the discipline will enter the club of sciences which are not altogether easy for outsiders to follow.

Any scientific theory has to work with precise concepts which by their very nature cannot coincide with the concepts of everyday life. No doubt the scientific language of individual disciplines will converge in the future forming a kind of theoretical and methodological *koine*. At present, however, every science has to care for its own terminology independently.

The problem of terminology cannot be conceived as being simply a question of choosing the right word; scientific terminology is not a linguistic problem. No word is 'right' in the case of a new concept which does not coincide with any concept of our everyday experience. The meanings of a set of words such as 'quality', 'trait', 'attribute' and 'property' are very close to each other in everyday speech (they are almost synonyms), yet they are used to denote different concepts in this volume. There are very few 'uncommitted' terms because the number of words of the natural language is limited, and an excessive use of Latin or Greek words makes the scientific language unpleasant even for its creators.

What I consider important is that the existing terminology and everyday usage of vocabulary should be retained wherever possible. I apologize for not having been entirely successful in realizing this point in practice. Feeling that it is the concepts that matter, I do not insist upon any of the special terms used in this book.

I dedicate the present volume to the memory of my father Jiří Neustupný, who was a strong and positive influence during the early days of my archaeological career by his deep interest in archaeological theory and method.

Acknowledgements

My first attempt at explaining my views on archaeological methodology was read and commented upon by Luboš Peške and my wife Ludmila. A number of valuable comments on the typescript of this volume were supplied by Martin Kuna and some by my brother Jiří. As I did not follow all their suggestions, the responsibility remains only with those passages that gained through their intervention.

I have been greatly influenced, one way or another, by my Czechoslovak colleagues, with whom I shared the same archaeological community for so many years. The analysis of their writings has become a source of my inspiration.

1

Notes on archaeology, its theory and method

This chapter is introductory in the sense that it tries to explain some concepts as used later in the book. On the one hand, it deals with several rather general topics (e.g. the relation between archaeological objects and means) which I consider to be more theoretical than methodological; these topics will not be discussed in any of the following chapters in more detail. On the other hand, some of the problems included in the following paragraphs (such as induction and deduction) will be further developed in a number of later chapters. Both cases require a rather short handling of the matter, concentrated on generalities and on differences from what I consider to be the usual understanding of various basic concepts. In no case should this chapter be mistaken for a systematic exposure of problems connected with the notions introduced here.

Many scholars limit their conception of archaeology to the study of material remains, leaving the 'higher' levels of 'historical' or 'anthropological' knowledge to another branch of science called 'prehistory'. This might seem to be an innocent division of the discipline into two parts, were it not for the fact that it makes modelling, the most specific archaeological method, operate in at least three disciplines in any case of its application: after establishing a model in the realm of prehistory, which cannot be done without reference to another discipline with 'observable time', one has to cross the boundary of prehistory into 'archaeology'; having tested the model by means of archaeological facts one has to return to the source of models via 'prehistory' to enrich the model and so on. And because the use of models is indispensable for any archaeological endeavour (i.e. from the phase of analysis), it means trespassing constantly across the two boundaries.

The concept of prehistory would appear logical only if it were conceived as *archaeological theory* based not only on the knowledge derived from the archaeological evidence but also on all outside knowledge obtained by sciences with observable time. Prehistory would then become the source of models used by archaeology; I wonder whether any such prehistory exists at present, and I am not sure whether it is logical to try to establish it as a particular discipline. The parallel with the seemingly analogous pair, archaeology–history, makes the problem even more complicated. Anyway, prehistory in this conception could not be understood as a counterpart to archaeology: the relation between the two disciplines would rather correspond to the relation of the empirical and the theoretical aspects of a single science.

It is, of course, impractical to view archaeology and prehistory as two separate sciences, but it could be tolerated were it not for the fact that such a conception of archaeology also has another, more serious, consequence for the methodology of our discipline. If archaeology is the study of material remains left behind by ancient man, and prehistory is another discipline, then models obviously need not be discussed within archaeological methodology; it might seem, in fact, that their use does not belong to archaeology at all. And this assumption again makes it easy to believe that, in the absence of models, archaeology in the narrow conception is able to generate 'prehistorical' knowledge or, to put it in other words, to believe that the historical process can be *observed* by means of archaeological finds. There are examples of such reasoning in the field of archaeological methodology (e.g. Hensel, Donato, and Tabaczyński 1986).

1.1   Archaeological objects and means

To define archaeology one has to analyse two methodologically important concepts: objects and means of a discipline. The *object* is the part of the real world towards which the discipline is directed while the *means* represents the sets of things or beings which become the immediate subject of inquiry. These two concepts were introduced to archaeology by a Ukrainian archaeologist, L. Zakharuk, in the sixties and have subsequently been discussed by several other authors (cf. Gening 1983).

There are many branches of science where the two elements, the means and the objects, fuse; in order for this to happen, it is necessary that a number of conditions are fulfilled. Some disciplines, such as many fields of biology or pre-nuclear physics, study their objects more or less directly – they simply observe them – and some are even able to experiment with them. In most instances like these the objects and the means of the particular disciplines are identical. The direct approach to the objects has two aspects:

(1) *observability* either by naked eye or by means of a simple sense-amplifier such as an optical microscope;
(2) observability of changes *over time.*

If a discipline is to be experimental, two additional conditions must be fulfilled:

(3) the *accessibility* of objects, and
(4) the availability of material means and energy sufficient to cause *changes* in the objects or in the conditions of their existence.

There is no doubt that archaeology is not an experimental science as the human past is not accessible to modern activities; it is impossible to exert any influence on historical conditions such that we would be able to observe the results. What has been called 'experimental archaeology' is only superficially similar to experimental disciplines in the natural sciences as it operates outside the time limits to which the archaeological record once belonged, and outside the conceptual world of ancient people.

It is impossible to compare the archaeological record with the contents of the so-called 'black box' as some would have it (cf. Clarke 1968, p. 59). The internal structure of such a black box, being inaccessible to direct observation, is discovered by manipulating its inputs and observing the reactions (outputs). In the case of archaeological records, however, no reaction can be expected at the output in response to anything that could be imagined as input. If any analogy can be drawn, then it is with an amber cube (or 'amber box') cut out of a piece of prehistoric resin and containing remains of an ancient insect: its material structure, however incomplete, can be more or less reliably observed (as is also the case in archaeology) but there is no way of affecting it experimentally. The amber box has neither inputs nor outputs.

If archaeology cannot be considered to be an experimental discipline, can it at least observe its objects over their own time? Irrespective of the question whether the object of archaeology is 'the finds' or the past processes, it is obvious that the time in which archaeologists are interested elapsed long ago. Archaeological observations take place in our modern time, which is quite different from that in which ancient artifacts and their users lived. The only possible way of removing this difficulty would be the acceptance of the thesis that archaeological objects are equivalent to antiquities with no recoverable relation to past life. Assuming this, such antiquities would be observed in their own time (which would then be our present) but they would be degraded to the role of *objet trouvé*. I am not going to discuss this kind of archaeology in the present volume. Clearly, the thesis that the object of archaeology is identical with its means cannot be upheld if archaeology is to be concerned with the past. What, then, are the means and what are the objects of our discipline?

The first part of the question is easier to answer. The *archaeological means* are represented by the record irrespective of how it is conceived. It can be observed (the observation includes its spatial and formal properties), but it is devoid of the time coordinate and, as a result, it is not accessible to our practice other than just the observation. Yet it constitutes the empirical basis of archaeology.

It is somewhat more complicated with the *object of archaeology*. Without going into detailed discussion of the most varied views proposed by many archaeologists throughout the world, I present the solution which I personally consider the most satisfying. The object of archaeology is the past process or, to be more exact, the *historical process* in human societies. This concept includes not only abstract regularities or laws of human behaviour in the past, but also the concrete manifestations of these laws as affecting real human groups (and their individual members) living at a specific place at a specific date and having a specific culture. I hope that such a position does not give up on any important aspect of the past.

The object of archaeology, i.e. the historical process, cannot be observed. It is known to have been dynamic (it took place in time) and to have been concrete (rich in details). The historical process constitutes the theoretical component of archaeology. *The archaeological method can be conceived as a set of procedures that lead from the record to the process*, i.e. from empirical to theoretical knowledge.

The means are sometimes called *sources* in historical sciences. Archaeology has its 'material' sources and history has its 'written' sources. This simple analogy might lead to the conclusion that the nature of the two kinds of 'sources' is similar. It is obviously impossible to experiment with the past on the basis of written records (just as it is impossible to experiment with the 'material' record), but there is a great difference between archaeology and history in that the records of the latter do contain observation taking place in time. This is the logical consequence of the fact that historical sources consist of language constructs which have the capacity of expressing both time change and causal explanation (however deformed it might be). Consequently, the written records are able to describe the historical process directly. The principal difference between a biologist observing his animals and a historian 'observing' the past through his records is that the historian is limited to what his source happened to note: the columns of his observation diary have been filled by another person, may not be objective, and not to the desirable degree, but they are present there. History based on written sources has its own difficulties but they differ in principle from those encountered by archaeology.

In the course of the advancement of human knowledge particular scientific disciplines have apparently formed on the basis of both their object and/or their means. Archaeology is one of those sciences which became specific on the basis of their means; this does not mean, however, that the object would be less important. *Archaeology is the science of man that studies the historical process on the basis (or by means) of archaeological records*. It shares its object with other historical disciplines. We shall, of course, return to the delimitation of the archaeological record in later paragraphs.

It is necessary to point out that in defining archaeology one has to include both the aspect of object and that of means. Archaeology is not simply the science of the archaeological record as in such a case, being a purely formal discipline, it would lose any meaning for contemporary mankind. At the same time, it is not simply a science of human history; the same objective is also approached by many other disciplines. Without stressing the role of the record (the means), archaeology could fall into the trap of dilettantism which does not respect its specific methodology.

1.2   Archaeological theory and archaeological method

The distinction between theory and method is not a straightforward one. The difficulties connected with the delimitation between the two aspects of science cannot be removed by any simple means such as formal definitions because, in the course of our cognition of the reality, theoretical constructs become methodological tools and vice versa. Thus, for example, models (which serve as methodological concepts in the course of interpretation) become parts of theory if successfully tested against the structure of archaeological finds; as we shall see later in this book, however, the same theory which results from the models, is subsequently turned back into models to become methodological means in another iteration of archaeological research. The difference between theory and method thus becomes a highly relative matter.

In spite of this, everybody feels that there is a distinction. Some problems are treated in contemporary archaeology predominantly as methodological and others predominantly as theoretical questions. The former group clearly includes, among other topics, analysis and what will be later described as the synthesis of archaeological structures; the latter group covers the discussion of recognized structures (such as particular cultural groups or chronological periods) and, of course, the concepts and categories resulting from the interpretation of the archaeological record. The two parts of

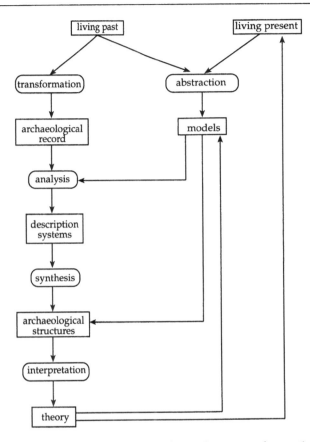

Fig. 1.1 The interdependence between theoretical and methodological steps

archaeology (i.e. theory and methodology) are clearly not identical in concrete research situations.

One way of distinguishing between theory and method is to conceive of the former as partial *results* of the cognitive process while the latter is understood as *ways* leading to the results. This is no strict definition but it often helps in making the distinction. The idea has been summarized in Fig. 1.1, where 'theory' appears in rectangles while 'methodology' is enclosed in oval rings. Most pairs of rectangles (those relevant to archaeology) have been joined through a ring which contains the name of the methodological procedure enabling the transition between two sets of theoretical problems.

This conception of the difference between archaeological theory and methodology is quite similar to that proposed by Pałubicka and Tabaczyński (1986). According to them, theory consists of hypothetical statements reflecting the structure of reality and the mechanisms of its change. Thus, theory includes not only the results of research but also the conceptual apparatus; consequently, theory becomes a 'research tool'. *While the object of archaeological theory consists of prehistoric phenomena themselves, the object of archaeological methodology consists of statements relating to those phenomena.* It follows that methodology discusses the ways in which statements about the past should be constructed; this again brings it near to Gardin's 'theoretical archaeology' (Gardin 1979).

The new directions in archaeology invading the discipline in the last twenty years or so have been predominantly theory orientated. There were, no doubt, important methodological themes discussed as well (such as the role of deduction vs. induction) but, on the whole, methodology was identified with the particular natural scientific or mathematical tools used in generating some aspects of archaeological knowledge.

It may not have been a chance development that the so-called New Archaeology stressed so much the deductive method; it was exactly in this way that its predominant occupation with theory became logical. Namely, if deduction from theoretical premises is the principal procedure for deriving archaeological theses, then it is theory that becomes important. Deduction, however, is more or less a logical method; archaeological facts, which are opposed to this method, can be preprocessed by means of the 'methodological' tools such as, for example, so-called statistical methods. It seems to me that some of the New Archaeologists were afraid that methodology, if followed beyond the level of research tools, could become harmful, bringing back some form of induction.

If, however, the methodolial constituent of our discipline is equated with the various research tools (such as dendrochronology, seriation and geomagnetic prospecting), then methodology falls out of the scientific endeavour unless some of its parts are included among the theoretical problems. It is interesting to note that the idea of replacement of archaeological method with research tools is shared by both empirically orientated archaeologists and their theoretical colleagues.

Looking nearer at the 'research tools' it becomes obvious that they do not, in fact, generate any theoretical statements on our record. What they do generate is a deeper, often more sophisticated, description of the finds and certain relations between them. The radiocarbon method states how much radioactive carbon a sample contains, and this is interpreted in terms of the time elapsing since a particular prehistorical event. The history of radiocarbon dating makes it clear that this interpretation is no simple process, depending not only on certain natural scientific premises but also on a number of archaeological assumptions (mainly that the death of the organic tissue in the sample is contemporaneous with the event to be dated). Similarly, chemical analysis of archaeological materials, if they are to be interpreted in terms of theoretical statements, rely on assumptions about the purposeful behaviour of ancient people. Generally speaking, natural scientific 'methods' require archaeological *methods* to generate theoretical statements of archaeological relevance; it is a frequent source of misunderstanding to believe that they do it automatically by themselves.

1.3 Deduction and induction

Traditional archaeology has inherited inductivist methodology from the nineteenth-century natural sciences. It was considered 'logical' to compile finds until they disclosed some aspects of antiquity. The regularities contained in the record and subsequently their interpretation grew up logically from the assembled and described facts: knowledge on generalities was obtained by putting together particular instances of archaeological phenomena. It should be noted at once that doing archaeology does *appear* like this procedure; many practitioners of archaeology would probably insist that they were successful proceeding in accordance with this inductivist recipe.

Inductivist methodology implied that all knowledge came

from generalizing based on sets composed of individual facts; if the facts failed to report on some aspect of ancient life, this may have been caused either by a complete disappearance of the relevant record or, more probably, by an insufficient quantity of the record. In many cases it seemed to be meaningful to dig until the desired 'sources' appeared in sufficient quantities. This philosophy led archaeologists to go on excavating throughout their lives in the belief that the record would begin speaking one day. It was considered to be bad scientific behaviour to exploit generalities obtained from a non-archaeological sphere; deduction was assumed to have its proper place in mathematics but not in the realm of 'concrete' sciences.

A reaction to these one-sided views was started by Binford in the early phases of the New Archaeology (Binford 1972). He conceded that the archaeological facts did not speak to him at all, irrespective of their number and the thoroughness of their description. He concluded that it was necessary to set up certain premises from which it might be possible to deduce consequences testable by means of archaeological finds. This is a logical procedure contrary to what the New Archaeologists described as the *narrow inductivism* of their opponents. The theoretical basis for these views was found within a logical discipline called the 'philosophy of science', but a rather narrow selection of readings on the theme was used (cf. Eggert 1978).

In spite of these limitations, Binford's criticism of inductivism was revolutionary as it opened new outlooks on the relationships between individual facts and general theory. In the framework of the deductive method it became possible to ask any question: the only problem involved was whether the set of general premises concerning the question (the hypothesis) allowed the deduction of a corresponding set of consequences which would be testable by means of the archaeological record. If the required facts were not at hand, it was possible to go out to the field to perform excavations aimed specifically at answering the questions posed by the hypothesis. Binford proposed to excavate not to find something unexpected but to find facts on which previously formulated hypotheses could be tested.

The question arises how the inductivists of the traditional archaeology could arrive at anything at all if their methodological basis did not include these principles. The answer is quite simple: they did not keep to their methodological assumptions as strongly as they, no doubt, themselves believed. They must have admitted theory to creep in, in the form of 'obvious' theses and/or hidden assumptions. For example, the inductivists proved richness to occur in a prehistoric society on the basis of elaborate grave furniture; in fact, they first deduced from a 'hidden' theory that richness could be reflected in an elaborate grave furniture and then concluded that their graves fulfilled this condition and therefore could be termed rich.

When the role of deduction in archaeology became firmly established, it may have seemed that induction was no more needed. As far as I know, such a conclusion was not defended theoretically but in practice many archaeologists tried to exploit the newly 'discovered' methodological principle to the utmost. This was, no doubt, a positive development after so many decades of inductivist pretensions, but the neglect of induction also had an adverse influence on archaeological methodology: those parts of the method which were predominantly inductive were not systematically developed. What will be described as the synthesis of structures in later chapters was left out, presumably for this reason; as a result, it seemed that it was 'raw' facts that were to be explained by means of 'hypotheses'.

The indisputable fact that already description is theory dependent (Neustupný 1971) does not remove its overwhelmingly inductive nature. The result of description, the descriptive systems, can be viewed as a generalized reflection of individual finds (they consist no more of things but of entities). In consequence of this, one part of analysis represents a movement from the individual to the general and can be characterized as an inductive procedure.

It is even more the case with archaeologial synthesis which begins with the descriptive systems and ends with structures. It is very obvious in this case that our knowledge of structures is a movement towards greater generality; at the same time there are very few generalities from which something needs to be deduced during the process of the generation of archaeological structures. As a result, the step of synthesis is even more inductive than description.

The situation is different with interpretation. Modelling, by means of which it is achieved, clearly involves the way from some general knowledge (a theory) to specific instances of the theory; consequently it employs mostly deductive reasoning. This may be the main reason why the early New Archaeologists, who were preoccupied with explanatory problems, also stressed the importance of the deductive method.

Apparently, induction and deduction belong among those pairs of concepts where neither the one nor the other extreme can be erased. Once scientists try to do so, the effect is harmful to the scientific method: the concept believed to be ousted returns through the back gate and becomes uncontrollable. It should be pointed out, while assessing the relative weight of induction as opposed to deduction, that there is hardly any step of the archaeological method where one of the two opposing logical procedures would be exclusive.

1.4   Empirical facts and theory

Empirical facts of archaeology are called finds; they are usually obtained in the field by means of excavations but some of them are simply discovered in museum collections. Empirical facts are highly esteemed by certain archaeological circles, more exactly by those archaeologists who spend most of their time in the field. Their positive judgement of the finds is often accompanied by a not very high appreciation of archaeological theory. This is fully in line with the situation in the nineteenth-century natural sciences which, being empirically orientated, considered their 'hard facts' to be the only firm basis for the solution of any questions of interest. While theories constantly change, explain the empirically orientated archaeologists, the finds remain the immutable basis for future reference. Those who obtain new 'materials' will be praised by all the archaeological generations to come while theoreticians will be forgotten after one or two decades.

This euphoria of the empiricists appears in a somewhat gloomy perspective once it becomes obvious that excavations, being theory dependent, do not usually bring materials other than those pertinent to the solution of questions asked by that theory. Those who engage in rescue excavations will certainly be praised in the future but other excavators would do better to take consolation in the fact that it is usually considered unfair to judge history (including the history of one's own discipline).

The empirical approach to archaeology is mostly combined with 'narrow' induction; this may produce very exact formal knowledge in some instances but hardly any explanation of the historical process. It is, of course, impossible to do without any theoretical premises, so some sort of 'hidden' non-empirical assumptions are necessarily introduced even by the most stubborn opponents of theory.

It has to be admitted that there are nowadays few archaeologists who oppose theory in principle. There are many, however, who believe that the archaeological finds contain everything that later appears in archaeological theory. This is to say otherwise that the finds uniquely determine the theory, which is another form of empiricism. Such a relationship between facts and theory would not be possible even if archaeology were not interested in process, as any scientific theory requires not only facts to be built but also some kind of preceding theory. The interests of present-day archaeology, however, make it more difficult to believe in the simple determination of theory by facts as anything concerning process presupposes the time coordinate, which is unobservable by archaeological means. This question will be discussed in later chapters in greater detail.

A sound relationship between facts and theory is also hampered by the historically originating situation which created not only specialists in excavations but also specialists in archaeological theory. The latter rarely say that finds are unnecessary (which would be a mischievous revenge taken on the 'excavators') but very many of them have been recently using finds as mere examples for their theories. When used this way, archaeological facts lose the role of sources of knowledge and means of testing theories; they become three-dimensional material illustrations for products of human brains. Sometimes, however, the finds seem to be in fact two-dimensional illustrations, as the theoreticians using them do not appear to take the third dimension into consideration, the finds being for them identical with line drawings in a publication.

In reality, facts and theory are interrelated in any branch of science. New knowledge cannot be obtained otherwise than by means of facts ('finds' in archaeology) but this cannot be done otherwise than by using theory intensively. How this is done in archaeology will be described in chapter 6.

1.5   Things and structures

When Ferdinand de Saussure at the beginning of this century distinguished between language and speech (*langue* and *parole* in the original French text), he started a new paradigm for many social sciences. Archaeology was little touched in spite of being invited to cooperate in the movement (J. V. Neustupný 1958). It was only in the late sixties that de Saussure's original theory was exploited to some degree (Deetz 1967) and Lévi-Strauss's interpretation of de Saussure was imported into the discipline (Hodder 1982, 1986) at a time when the structuralist paradigm had already been overcome in linguistics (cf. J. V. Neustupný 1978).

De Saussure's original idea (1974) has mostly been interpreted in the following way: it is necessary to distinguish between 'speech' (the sounds or written signs which form the 'palpable', material side of the process of human communication) and the pattern of the process, its system, which is called language. It is language that is the subject of linguistics. The objects which structure language (the phonemes, for example) are arbitrary (their material manifestation resembles in no way their meaning) and formal (it is only their formal oppositions that matter). While language is abstract and formal (in the sense outlined above) but logical, speech is concrete, significant and historical.

The same difference apparently applies to the world of archaeological concepts. There is an archaeological 'language' as well as an archaeological 'speech'. The former became the main topic within the New Archaeology which, however, did pay attention to the *meaning* of archaeological patterns; in this respect it transcended pure structuralism, approaching the sociolinguistic paradigm of linguistics. The so-called post-processual archaeology, if I understand the movement well, works towards the understanding of the archaeological 'speech', i.e. mainly the significance and historicity of the past process. This is, no doubt, a positive development, if it is not claimed that this sort of study should replace (not supplement) the endeavour of previous archaeological generations. From the point of view of this book it should be noted that the methodology of significance and history has not yet been established and, in consequence of this, post-processual archaeology cannot boast concrete results that could persuade those who do not yet believe.

The idea of distinguishing pairs of concepts such as 'language' and 'speech' is certainly not entirely new, and those acquainted with the philosophy of the eighteenth and nineteenth centuries will probably be able to identify its sources. De Saussure, however, seems to be the first to have applied these ideas to a concrete discipline using it as a methodological tool. Although they developed within structural linguistics, their application within post-structural paradigms is fully justified and, indeed, necessary.

It is not very important which words are used to refer to the equivalents of language and speech in archaeology but it is extremely important to realize that such a distinction exists. Both the facts and the structures are real. On the one hand, each archaeological fact has an internal structure which can be explained as its pattern, rule or law (several facts have the same structure in common); on the other hand, structures, being abstractions, do not exist otherwise than in things. It follows that structures are rules (or laws) contained in facts.

De Saussure, in spite of considering his 'language' to be the only object of linguistics, did not deny that the other aspects of human speech should be studied scientifically. In fact, however, neither he nor his followers cared to work in fields other than structuralist 'language'; as a result they denied the importance of those fields in practice. A change came only within the new paradigm of sociolinguistics (J. V. Neustupný 1978).

Some points made by proponents of the typological paradigm in archaeology stand quite close to the views of structuralists, for example their preoccupation with formal relations
among archaeological entities as well as abstraction from
meaning in the framework of the diffusion theory. The new,
post-typological paradigm, with its interest in the relation of
the archaeological record to the other parts of culture and the
social sphere in general, can be compared – at least in this
respect – to sociolinguistics.

On the whole, however, archaeology was not the kind of
environment where a sort of linguistic structuralism could
flourish. Its record was so concrete, and its contacts with
history (of whatever brand) were so close. This may be the
reason why the theory of diffusion never developed into
archaeological structuralism; as we shall see in chapter 3, there
was always a strong feeling (at least in the Old World) that
archaeology has to do with history, which resulted in the
survival of migrations and evolution side by side with diffusion.

1.6   The role of mathematics

In the view of many archaeologists mathematics is just
another discipline, such as zoology or physics, with which it is
useful to cooperate from time to time. I shall try to argue in the
following paragraphs that this view is not exact.

Archaeologists always counted and measured their finds
and, once their science became more developed, they also
calculated percentages. From the present day retrospective,
this phase looks like the prehistory of the application of
mathematics. There were some interesting attempts in the
first half of the twentieth century, but more complicated
mathematical methods were not introduced before the fifties.
Then, an outburst followed in the sixties being already closely
connected with the new theoretical currents of that time.

The first attempts at using more complicated mathematics
were still connected with traditional problems (chronological
ordering by means of seriation) but soon it was used for the
solution of 'new' questions (Binford and Binford 1966). It was
typical of this early phase that mathematical methods were

not sought in mathematics but in other 'concrete' sciences which had already progressed to a higher stage of 'applying' mathematics (psychology, biology, geography etc.). Sokal and Sneath's numerical taxonomy became a programme for many archaeologists.

It was often argued that the necessity of using mathematics (or statistics, as it was sometimes termed) followed from the great quantities of archaeological finds which could no more be handled effectively without a recourse to complicated quantitative methods. It is surprising that this myth is still current despite the fact that already the first successful applications of mathematics dealt with rather small samples. Almost all the seriations, correlation analyses, factor analyses etc., as well as most of the statistical tests, were made on samples of small or medium size. Up to the present comparatively few really large archaeological contexts have been analysed by means of mathematics. Clearly, the quantity of finds was an excuse for something else.

The concern for quantity as the explanation for using mathematics appears to be a natural consequence of viewing it exclusively as a science of numbers. In connection with this viewpoint it is often accepted that the qualitative aspect of the archaeological method should be the subject of 'pure' archaeology while the quantitative side of the problem may require some help from the side of mathematics. This conception of the role of mathematics, however, is untenable: mathematics is concerned with both the 'quantitative' and the 'qualitative' aspects of things, and the same is true about archaeology.

Thus, for example, there is nothing particularly quantitative about the mapping of a set of archaeological objects into a set of archaeological descriptors; the relation of incidence, e.g. an incidence of beakers and battle-axes in graves of a Corded Ware cemetery, is a purely qualitative concept (unless we need a measure of incidence). A factor of 'factor analysis' is a set of archaeological descriptors ordered by means of the corresponding 'factor loadings' but the loadings are not the exclusive results of the method: the set of the descriptors is equally important.

It is not mere numbers, but the most *abstract structures* of our world, that mathematics is about. It describes how things are ordered, how they function and how they change. By the way, ordering, interdependence and change are the most basic concepts of modern mathematics; its (partial) ordering, however, is so abstract that it may not resemble the concept of order in the social sciences, and the same may be true about 'functions' and dynamic systems.

The preceding paragraphs are not to say that mathematics, as practised at present, is able to express any complicated social structures and their functioning; it has been developed mainly to model the world of physics, which is much more simple than the human world.

But if mathematics is conceived in its role of a theory of abstract structure, its role in archaeology cannot be the same as in physics or biology. The latter groups of sciences have their own objects, but the object of mathematics as used in archaeology and the object of archaeology are the same. As a result, archaeologists themselves have to master mathematical means to be able to study their records from the structural point of view. The requirement to engage mathematicians on a large scale is about the same as to ask logicians to cooperate in compiling site reports on the pretext of making them more logical. Mathematics is contained in the object of archaeology to the same degree as in the objects of other scientific disciplines.

This does not mean that archaeologists should try to replace mathematicians in their proper tasks of developing new mathematical theories, proving their theorems (which is a favourite occupation of one brand of mathematicians) or devising algorithms for calculations. Archaeologists should become well-informed and conscious users of mathematics; this is a requirement that presupposes some additional effort on the side of both disciplines.

It cannot be denied that archaeologists have to study far more mathematics than they were used to one generation ago. Their endeavour to master mathematics, however, should be orientated to the comprehension of its methodological aspects. This is a point where mathematicians should cooperate by creating text-books free of problems specific to students of their own speciality (proofs etc., most of which are unnecessary to those who simply want to understand the sense of the discipline). Also, most of the algorithms of numerical mathematics and the formulas used for the calculation of statistical tests have now become dispensable.

These new requirements demand considerable changes in mathematics itself, which would come anyway: modern personal computers are turning it into a tool for everybody. This is an interesting development even in comparison with the period of mainframe computers when mathematics are still the preserve of the few who either could use the services of an experienced programmer or were able to write programs themselves. This period is now being overcome and mathematics is becoming, for the first time in its history, the object of concern for all scientists. What is still required on the side of the non-mathematician is the understanding of principles and the knowledge of how to use the results.

Of course, modern computers make it easy to misuse mathematics by applying some of its sophisticated methods to improper data or the like, but it is clear that any tool can be misused one way or another.

2

Prerequisites of the
archaeological method

If archaeologists are to study the historical process they must
have at their disposal certain prerequisites which are generally assumed to consist of the record. I would argue that the
second component of these preliminaries, the paradigm, is
equally important. Strictly speaking, neither the records nor
the paradigms are methodological concepts (they rather
belong to archaeological theory); the reason why they are
discussed in more detail at this point can be explained by the
fact that this pair of concepts mediates between the pair
'objects-means' and a series of other pairs of methodological
tools such as 'deduction-induction' or 'models-structures'
described previously.

2.1 Archaeological records

Typically, the archaeological record is classified
according to the assumed function of its constituents into
groups such as pottery, tools, weapons, personal ornaments,
animal bones, etc. This is undoubtedly a valid division, as it is
also the case of the difference between, for example, the
mobile and the immobile evidence. These divisions, however,
may not express properly what seems to be most important
for contemporary archaeology.

First of all we have to define the archaeological record to
distinguish it from the non-archaeological component of the
modern world: this is an important task as traces of human
activity seem to be ubiquitous on the surface of the Earth. We
shall classify *any material object containing some non-written
information on the human past such that it no longer serves its
original purpose* as part of the archaeological record. By means

of this definition we set apart written records which consist of signs and, of course, any objects of nature with no direct connection with the human past. For reasons of completeness it should be remarked that the information recorded on modern audio-visual tapes and discs and/or similar media for computers, etc. also does not belong to the archaeological record. To be excluded too are all objects produced in the past but still possessing their original function as well as all con-temporary man-made things, mainly modern artifacts and modern waste, which do not contain any *direct* information about the past. The word 'direct' should be stressed in this connection as almost any system of the contemporary world can be used *indirectly* as a source of knowledge on history; this is a natural consequence of the fact that the contemporary world is a development of the past.

The preceding paragraph will hardly be acceptable to those who insist upon a purely empirical approach to science. Our definition contains reference to the information which, in the view of many, should be obtained from the record itself and should not be supposed in advance. The point argued in this book is that there is no way of recognizing a part of the modern world as a possible archaeological means other than an assumption based on previous knowledge. In fact, by assuming the capacity of a material object to inform us about a former state of past peoples we accept a kind of model, although a very simple and a very abstract one.

Positivist scientists approached the archaeological record (as any other scientific means) as outside objects which can be observed but which are unknown prior to the observation. It was a severe sin against the scientific method to know some-thing about one's record in advance of its analysis. Here we come across the apparent fact that the archaeologist must know a lot about his record well in advance of its study: in addition to assuming that some sorts of things contain in-formation about past mankind he has to accept, for example, that the things he is going to observe have been created intentionally and that they had some form and function; otherwise he would not be able to determine them as human artifacts.

Despite the fact that some archaeologists do not exclude the contemporary material remains of man from the archaeological record, I still believe that archaeology is about the past. This is not so much because of the etymology of the word (αρχαιος) as because of the specificity of archaeology which has always been concerned with *dead remains* of the past. (This aspect of archaeology will be discussed in chapter 3 in more detail.) It is interesting to note that humanity has established a scientific subdiscipline for the study of almost any part of nature or technology. However, as far as I know, nobody has ever attempted to create any *comprehensive theory of contemporary human artifacts and other products*: the whole world of man-made things that nowadays cover ever larger areas of the Earth's surface remains without a theoretical coverage. Archaeology can hardly make up for this deficiency but, I believe, it can greatly contribute to its creation. Archaeologists, at least, would be among the first to profit from the advances of such a science. My hopes in this respect are espoused by the fact that the theory of artifacts must necessarily include their dynamic aspects – something that archaeologists need for constructing their models but are unable to supply on the basis of their own records.

Many handbooks on archaeology maintain that archaeological records are material things and this is, of course, true. I do not see, however, how this fact could help in answering the basic question, namely what are archaeological remains and what are not. Most parts of the world that surrounds us are material. In contrast to this overwhelming material majority of our environment there stand out some works of art, many of them containing various symbols, which are clearly non-material but they are traditionally included in the scope of archaeology. (It is obvious that even the 'non-material', semiological components of human culture cannot do without *material carriers* such as papyrus scrolls or walls or pots.) Symbols and artistic images (icons) would not concern us here if it were not for the fact that they are clearly semiological objects.

It might be asked, in this connection, whether the differences between natural language on the one side and symbols and icons on the other are sufficient to draw a line between them. I believe that the principal difference lies in the fact that symbols and icons are, in contrast to the signs of language, not ordered either in time or in space; it is rare to obtain their uniquely interpreted sequence (such as a series of scenes depicting a logically continuous series of events). As a result, symbols and icons have no true grammar, as grammar cannot do without an ordered set of elements. In the absence of such an order, symbols and icons are unable to express any kind of dynamics; thus they occupy the same position as any other group of the archaeological record.

There are other good reasons for accepting symbols and images into archaeology. It is not only tradition and the fact that there is no other branch of science to discuss them, it is also some of the properties of symbols such as their semi-arbitrary nature which necessitates their archaeological study. This is to say, in other words, that the forms of symbols and images may in some way imitate cultural or natural things; to recognize them as objects having some meaning requires a good orientation in their environment or context (cf. Hodder 1986), a task which can hardly be accomplished without deep archaeological knowledge and without the use of complicated archaeological methods. The same is true of the process of recovering the significance of 'material' objects: the necessity of taking into consideration the culture as a whole is also obvious. It is difficult to imagine how these tasks could be performed outside of archaeology.

Many text-books on archaeology also maintain that the specific property of the archaeological record lies in the fact that it has been excavated from the earth. This is again almost correct but there are many monuments such as the megaliths, pyramids, etc. whose major parts have never been buried; yet, they belong to archaeology. Many 'excavated' objects, however, such as trilobites, are of no archaeological concern. To characterize the archaeological record as the testimony of the 'buried past' is not exact; it may have been tempting because it seems to supply a clear-cut empirical criterion for the decision whether a thing belongs to the archaeological record or not. Such a decision can hardly be reached on the basis of the observed evidence alone.

Some of the possible divisions of the archaeological record have already been mentioned. The problem was a favourite topic of traditional methodology and some authors have developed schemes going into considerable detail and insight (Childe 1956). The following paragraphs contain yet another classification partly derived from the opposition between artifacts and ecofacts as known from the writings of the New Archaeology in the 1960s (Binford 1964 and many others). I believe that the scheme presented here reflects a set of principles which are not entirely surface phenomena within what remained from the past.

2.1.1   The artifactual record

It is a common property of the artifactual record that its elements have been *intentionally formed to become means of some human activity or purpose*. The human goal, whether pertaining to the economic, social or ideological sphere, gives to the constituents of the artifactual record formal properties which are very improbable in natural objects: their *entropy* is low. At the same time people, acting within a living culture, tend to place them in spatial clusters and this further diminishes their entropy. In addition to artifacts the group of artifactual records includes 'complexes' (not very ingeniously described as 'assembled finds') and 'components'. The artifactual record is the traditional domain of archaeology which has been attracting the attention of the majority of archaeologists until recent decades. The empirically observed form of artifacts, the complexes and components, are usually described as archaeological remains, monuments, sites or simply as finds. Traditional archaeology rarely reached beyond the complexity of complexes, and in some countries even this concept has remained more or less unused until quite recently.

It is obvious that we have to assume much knowledge about our finds to be able to describe them as pieces of the artifactual record. In the course of a first approach to archaeological finds this knowledge cannot be obtained otherwise than by means of a consensus among specialists; but this tacit agreement, which takes the place of the first (preliminary) model, cannot be considered to be a valid theory of the finds. It must be followed by steps of analysis and synthesis as described in chapters 4 and 5. We should perhaps mention the seductive idea that artifacts could possibly be identified, instead of using the consensus, by analysing and measuring the entropy of the finds. This is, unfortunately, not feasible. If we were to measure entropy, it would be necessary, among other things, to establish a set of properties of the material objects to be followed; and such a selection of properties would again be impossible without preliminary assumptions.

Artifacts are separate and undivided pieces of the archaeological record, i.e. objects intentionally formed to become means of human activity or a group of interconnected activities. As usual with definitions, this general statement presents some problems. Can a wheel be described as an artifact? In fact, it is generally a part of a waggon and, consequently, something like a fragment. Yet in the archaeological record it often appears separately. In general, it seems that fragments must be accepted as representatives of artifacts, otherwise there would be very few artifacts indeed. There are often problems with making sure that an object served as a means of human activity; it could have been just a piece of waste which does not respond to the definition of the artifact. Also, the intentionality of artifacts is far from certain in many instances. This is a well-known topic in the case of very early palaeolithic tools: were they tools at all? It is less well known that similar problems arise with much later monuments, for example with compact belts of stones surrounding some hills in Central Europe believed to be early iron age fortresses.

The definition of an artifact requires that it should serve some human activity or purpose. The 'activity or purpose' must be conceived here in the widest sense of the word: it is not only production, but also consumption; even religious rituals as well as any display of social prestige must be subsumed under this heading. Consequently, artifacts include chisels, knives and houses; bread and beer; various kinds of semi-finished products and raw materials; prehistoric 'Venuses' and toys for children; personal ornaments and symbolic weapons; stone stelae (but not the contents of the inscriptions they carry). Despite the fact that some lists of artifacts have been constructed with great care (e.g. Childe

1956), it is impossible for them to be complete. There is a tendency, observable during the evolution of human culture, to produce ever more types of artifacts; but even this tendency cannot be proved to be absolute.

For the greater part of the nineteenth century, archaeologists were concerned almost exclusively with isolated artifacts, not being aware of any higher-order class of their record. It was only the so-called typological paradigm that called attention to the fact that most artifacts occurred in clusters which, being reflections of past events, contained much additional information not included in their simple sum. The higher-order clusters have been variously named assembled finds, assemblages, closed finds and the like. The best examples are graves or subterranean houses. I am inclined to use the word *complex* to designate shortly this important archaeological category.

It is not by chance that the importance of complexes came to be recognized within the framework of the typological paradigm: the newly emergent question of fine chronology brought about the necessity of investigating more closely how artifacts had been deposited jointly.

It is important to realize that complexes are not simple aggregates of artifacts. A grave cannot be equated with the sum of grave goods it contains, not even with the grave goods *plus* the skeleton *and/or* the grave pit. It consists, in addition to its artifactual components, of their relationships which can be both formal and spatial. The grave is a whole, a *system* which cannot be reduced to a list of its elements.

Although the space occupied by a complex need not be delimited by clearly set boundaries, it is often the case: a grave is contained in its grave pit, a house has its walls, and a storage pit is also a confined space. The existence of containment may make it easier to identify a complex in many instances, but the decisive criterion for the recognition of a complex lies outside the realm of its formal or spatial properties: similarly, as in the case of simple artifacts, archaeologists again build on the basis of a certain kind of consensus. The inventory of a grave pit often includes earlier or later intrusions and it is frequently difficult to identify them as such on the basis of their formal and spatial properties alone.

It follows that it is the intentionality which is the important attribute of a complex: the intention of past people was vital for its formation and it would be impossible to identify it without taking the intentionality into consideration. Even unintentionally assembled complexes may carry some relevant information: this is because such aggregates are often remnants of true complexes.

The role of complexes in building fine-scale chronologies has already been mentioned. However, their importance in archaeology cannot be limited to this particular use. In general, they always reflect some *event or a series of events* like a burial, the erection, use and desertion of a house, etc. The coincidence of artifacts in a complex and their non-random spatial organization within its confines can be explained by the assumption that the complex served some purpose at some time in the past. Thus, complexes contain much more information than just chronological ordering.

While complexes have been known since the end of the last century, the still higher entities of the archaeological record, the *components* have not yet entered the archaeological dictionary on any large scale. The word has appeared several times in the American literature on the subject (e.g. Chang 1967) but the meaning there is somewhat different from the concept introduced here. What we call a component in this book is a set of artifacts and complexes at a site, coming from one period of time and serving one purpose. In consequence of this, the elements of components display a distinct formal and spatial structure. While complexes reflect events, *components reflect activities* performed at a site during a limited period of time. Each component can be connected with an activity whether economic, social or ideological, and each of these activity types may be reflected in several types of more specific activities (and, consequently, in several kinds of components). Many sites contain the dwelling component (usually consisting of houses or other dwelling objects) and the storing component (consisting of storage pits, barns, etc.); the latter may, but need not, coincide spatially with the dwellings. The burial component is most frequently situated in another place, though not a very distant one. Sanctuaries and mines are clearly other types of components; a hoard of

metal objects is to be understood as an independent component usually consisting of a single complex.

It is obvious that a predecessor of our 'component' concept
could be described as something like 'the class of complexes'
but, as far as I know, this has never been used as a stage in the
hierarchy of the archaeological record. Settlement sites, cemeteries, hoards, etc. always remained empirical categories on
the level of 'pure' or 'primary' observation and were rarely
given any methodological or theoretical meaning. Certain
kinds of components may be ignored. For example the agricultural production component has been discussed only in
regions with well-preserved ancient fields and has been completely neglected in regions with badly preserved empirical
evidence, despite the fact that agriculture was practised there.
The situation is even worse with components which could be
termed pasture. Thus, without the concept of components,
some parts of the archaeological record may be missed unless
they are represented by very suspicious archaeological
features.

One of the reasons why archaeologists have so far paid little
attention to components may lie in the fact that they apparently contain so much non-empirical information. In regions
such as Central Europe one site often consists of remains of
several occupations which are not chronologically contigu-
ous; to separate them into several components it is necessary
to reconstruct their exact chronology. Also, a common function has to be assumed for the set of archaeological features to
be included into one 'component'. Moreover, the condition of
'one site' for the recognition of a component apparently
expresses the idea of its being a reflection of a single community. All this does not seem too disturbing to me because, in
my opinion, the record includes some measure of non-
empirical knowledge anyway, but it may be an intellectual
obstacle for those who believe they must build exclusively on
'hard facts'.

Many archaeologists stress the role of the *site* in archaeological theory and method as it is often represented by a
clearly delimited spatial cluster of artifacts (cf. Chang 1967).
However, a site is frequently a rather superficial agglomerate
of antiquities covering periods of thousands of years and

difficult to circumscribe; such a situation is typical of those regions of the world where agriculture began early and led to at least some degree of dense population. The site is an empirical unit which in some cases can be observed 'objectively' but, on the whole, it is a rather bad starting point for analysing the archaeological record.

The site concept can be replaced with the concept of *settlement areas*, a not necessarily continuous set of components reflecting the life of one community. This concept works in the case of simple peasant societies but it may be difficult to apply to more developed forms of social life. A typical settlement area of prehistoric farmers consists of the following components: dwelling, storage, production (fields and pastures), possibly hunting, burial and other ritual components. There can be many other kinds of components such as mining areas and places of non-agricultural production (metallurgy, potting, etc.). It is worth noting that none of the components is able to display the culture as a whole; settlement areas of simple agricultural societies, however, often do possess this ability. The settlement areas are higher units of the archaeological record which allow archaeologists to study the structure of human activities.

One can easily imagine that complex societies produce more complicated types of archaeological record. Its units still await formulation; in fact, our theoretical knowledge of anything that surpasses the complexes is still inadequate.

2.1.2 *Ecofacts*

The New Archaeologists of the 1960s introduced a new concept called *ecofacts* (cf. Binford 1964). It has not yet entered into widespread usage in the literature and some archaeologists questioned its import (e.g. Kleyn 1978). Yet, I believe that the ecofacts constitute an important division of the archaeologial record.

Ecofacts are things of nature whose individual properties have been *unintentionally* changed by man. Their major difference from artifacts is in the fact that the latter have been changed *intentionally* to serve some human purpose. While artifacts are expressions of man the creator, ecofacts reflect the same man as a blind natural agent who changes his environment without having any intention of doing so. An archaeological object is frequently both an artifact and an ecofact, i.e. it may be intentionally shaped and, at the same time, its natural properties may be unwittingly changed.

As a result there are two classes of ecofacts. One of them is composed of things which have no intentional cultural form at all; unworked human or animal bones are examples of this category. The other class of ecofacts is formed by virtually all artifacts, more exactly by their unintentional properties imposed on them as a by-product of some human action. There is hardly any artifact which people would not turn into an ecofact in the second sense.

For example, prehistoric potters fixed the Earth's magnetic field (its intensity, declination, inclination and dip) in any of the numerous vessels which they fired to several hundred degrees centigrade. The potting clay has consequently become an ecofact. Producing charcoal of the fire wood or harvesting grain, prehistoric people stopped the exchange of C^{14} between the plants and the atmosphere and moved the remains of the plants to a human environment. Thus they caused the amount of radiocarbon in the plant tissues to diminish with passing time; the concentration of radiocarbon has become an ecofact of the first class.

Another example: ancient peasants, burning a forest plot to make their 'fields', helped to create the so-called cultural steppe by changing the biocoenoses for plants and animals; this was clearly an unwanted side-effect forming an ecofact. Human activity produces such phenomena almost daily; some of them did not go unnoticed by ancient peoples and were exploited by them for the refinement of their technology (for example, the origin of metallurgy is believed to have belonged to this class). But most of the by-products remained unknown to their producers and are only discovered by modern scientists.

For those who look exclusively for the formal 'attributes' or archaeological finds there is no difference between artifacts and ecofacts. As I see it, however, the contrast between the two classes of the archaeological record is important. Even leaving aside the theoretical opposition there is the indisputable fact that ecofacts (or ecofactual properties) should become the object of specialized study by natural scientists, not archaeologists. Much confusion can arise, and has already arisen, from archaeological incursions into natural sciences – though accomplished in the innocent belief that this or that method is simple and requires no theoretical and/or methodological background in a branch of biology, geophysics, etc.

Ecofacts are a comparatively recent addition to the archaeological vocabulary and their properties have not yet been studied. This applies not only to their recognition but mainly to their special role in further steps of the archaeological method. Many natural scientists approach ecofacts as if they were identical to any other object of their study, and archaeologists are mostly unqualified for the task.

2.1.3 *The natural facts*

The preceding paragraphs are not to say that every natural object found in connection with some archaeological context is necessarily an ecofact. There are certainly pieces of nature untouched by man but still containing archaeological information: consequently, such natural objects belong among the archaeological records. These are what will be described as *natural facts* in this book.

A part of the 'untouched' natural phenomena influenced ancient peoples in one way or another: it was, for example, the climate, the hydrology and geomorphology of the inhabited region, the flora and fauna in the uninhabited vicinity of prehistoric settlement areas, etc. The other part of the 'natural facts' did not influence the historical process at all but it has been found in spatial connection with the archaeological record. It may be, for example, botanical remains or animal bones in natural layers just below or above a palaeolithic site; they may help to date the site within a chronological sequence.

While the methods for the study of the ecofacts are, at least theoretically, unclear, the methodology of the study of the natural facts seems to present no problems: those parts of nature which are relevant in this case are purely natural objects and are to be studied by typical natural scientific methods (it should not be forgotten, however, that the natural scientists are faced with the same problem as archaeologists: their objects are dead, but this is not an unknown problem in palaeontology). Archaeologists may provoke interest in the study (or may even take some samples for the natural scientists) but they can hardly do more than take over the results and apply them to their needs.

2.2   Paradigms

As shown by Thomas Kuhn in 1962, the evolution of the natural sciences is guided by so-called paradigms. A number of archaeologists have explored the idea that similar paradigms also rule the development of archaeology. The paradigm is certainly a useful concept and its exploration has brought new insights into the history of our discipline despite the fact that it cannot be applied to archaeology with exactly the same content as suggested by Kuhn for the natural sciences.

Paradigms are sets of theoretical standards accepted as self-evident by a community of scientists during their scientific training. They determine the questions to be posed, the methods to be used, and they even suggest the 'right' kinds of solutions. The paradigms represent sets of unrecognized theoretical assumptions which the specialists who are *in* the paradigm consider so much self-evident that they do not formulate them explicitly; it is usually only when a paradigm is discarded that it becomes possible to analyse its assumptions. The rule of a paradigm does not end because it is disproved but simply because there are no more specialists willing to defend it; it dies out.

2.2.1   *The dying paradigm in archaeology*

Theoretical developments in archaeology since the sixties have made it possible to formulate the principal assumptions of the paradigm that ruled our discipline in the past. I shall refer to it as the 'typological' paradigm although it may well turn out that it was in fact a batch of several paradigms. It developed in the last quarter of the nineteenth century and went through a series of changes marked, in Europe, by names such as Montelius, Kossinna, Menghin and Childe. V. G. Childe became one of its first critics.

Archaeologists who worked within the typological paradigm were interested mainly in the artifactual record from which they picked out individual artifacts and complexes; higher units of the artifactual record remained unknown or at least unused at any larger scale. There was no particular interest in ecofacts.

The principal theoretical categories consisted of the concepts of type, culture (or cultural group) and period (stage or phase). The type was usually defined as a set of artifacts possessing common properties; it was frequently characterized either by a single attribute (e.g. many types of iron age fibulae) or by a group of a few attributes. The verbal definition of types, however, was often rather fuzzy, if there was any at all: it was replaced with a drawing or a photograph. The culture (culture group) was understood as a set of types repeatedly occurring in the same territory. The stage (period, phase) expressed chronological divisions.

The principal archaeological method was typology, which had been most persuasively formulated by Oscar Montelius in the last quarter of the nineteenth century. In a more general sense typology followed changes of types; the changes were interpreted either as evolution or as mutual influencing. The spatial distribution of finds was also taken into account. This led to the recognition of the importance of stratigraphy and to the mapping of type distributions believed to reflect the spread of types in one direction or another.

Modelling, which I shall describe in chapter 6, was unknown to the adherents of the typological paradigm. The knowledge obtained by means of typology, stratigraphy or the study of distributions was, of course, interpreted but this was mostly done either by means of simple analogy with ethnography or history, or by transferring whole ideologies (such as the Nazi ideology) on to the archaeological material.

The typological paradigm admitted a limited selection of problems. At the level of what I have described as archaeological means it was the reconstruction of types and their arrangement into typological series, the determination

of relative chronology by means either of typological considerations or of stratigraphy), the definition of the 'contents'
of individual cultural groups and phases (by assembling lists
of their types), the tracing of the origin of types and thereby
of the culture groups, and the settling of questions such
as whether the types originated by local development
(evolution) or by mixing of elements whose origin was heterogeneous (which implied an 'influence'). The following questions were asked on the level of interpretation (or the 'object'
of archaeology): whether the sources reflected a continuation
of an ethnic group at one place or whether a migration had
taken place; what was the origin of the individual ethnic
groups manifested in the archaeological record; and which
cultural currents (bringing the 'influences') had diffused the
individual cultural elements.

Answers permitted within the typological paradigm
differed according to which tradition or 'school' prevailed at
the place where the archaeologist worked or where he had
been brought up; the 'schools' have been sometimes
described as more or less independent paradigms. The basic
problem on which archaeologists differed was the explanation
of the variability of artifacts in time and space. Quite often
only one solution was admitted: migration of a foreign ethnic
group. This kind of reply was supplied by the so-called settlement archaeology or Kossinna's school, going back to the
pre-Nazi period in Germany, then fostered by the Nazis, but
influential (in a non-ideological form) in Central European
archaeology long after the end of World War II.

Another reply to the basic question was devised by the
Vienna cultural historical school which had its roots in ethno-
logy: at the beginning of history there had been several cultural spheres (*Kulturkreise*) on the Earth, and the whole development of human culture could be reduced to simple
combination of elements coming from these cultural spheres.
One of the principal concepts became 'diffusion', i.e. the
spread of cultural elements from the original centres.

The third most frequent type of answer was an evolutionist
explanation derived from the evolutionism of the nineteenth-
century natural sciences. Typological changes of artifacts
were understood as an analogy to the Darwinian evolution of
species. This intellectual environment was the birth-place of

the typological method and the Scandinavian countries
became a stronghold of this school.

Few archaeologists can be assigned to only one of the
'schools' without reserve as they usually admitted various
solutions for their individual problems. Also, taking Central
European archaeology as an example, we can observe that the
individual schools were differently influential in different
periods of prehistory: while the eneolithic period was the
realm of migrations, the following bronze age was seen as a
period where much could be explained by evolution.

Typological archaeology was a qualitative discipline: to
follow migrations, diffusion or typological evolution it was
unnecessary to consider the quantitative aspects of human
culture. The adverse attitude to quantity went so far that even
absolute chronology was considered unnecessary (and, in
fact, it was unimportant within the typological paradigm). It
may have been applied to the study of cultural influences over
great distances where relative chronology was unreliable.
Absolute chronology was used in contacts with laymen while
archaeologists communicated among themselves in terms of
relative stages.

At the very end of its rule, however, the typological paradigm did incorporate quantitative studies in such quantity
that certain publications of this kind can be mistaken for New
Archaeology. It is the application of numerical taxonomy and
of seriation (the mathematical reformulation of typology)
which is the most typical armament of this approach.

When the typological paradigm ruled our discipline,
archaeologists tended to specialize according to the spatial
and chronological context of the records they studied. One
was known to be a specialist in the neolithic of Greece while
his colleague was at home in the African iron age. There could
hardly be any other kind of specialization if the main question
was the explanation of the variability of the archaeological
record in terms of migrations, diffusion and/or typological
evolution. A person who would have chosen a theme such as,
for example, prehistoric cattle breeding, would have been
entirely useless in the framework of typological archaeology:
he could hardly have brought anything of importance to the
solution of problems considered as 'important'.

Let us note that field research was also heavily influenced

by the paradigm. It is clear that the search for ecofacts was a waste of time (possibly with the exception of human skulls which were believed to be useful in assessing the ethnic origin of the deceased and in tracing the migratory paths of the 'cultural group' in question). Exceptional and unique finds were admired (they were assumed to be sensitive indicators of routes of diffusion) while domestic pottery and production refuse were completely uninteresting and, consequently, could be thrown away.

2.2.2 *The sources of the typological paradigm*

The epistemological basis of the typological paradigm is partly rooted in the unsatisfactory state of human knowledge in general. The natural and technical sciences of the first half of the twentieth century could hardly extend the necessary help to archaeologists (for example by studying their ecofacts) as it was only by the fifties that they were beginning to reach a state of some usefulness for archaeology. Even if some of the scientific methods were known before the middle of the century, their mass application in the service of archaeology was unthinkable because of the undeveloped technology. Mathematics did not become attractive for archaeologists before the spread of non-parametric methods, and its use did not become widespread before the advent of computers, without which it could hardly be applied on any larger scale; the process of computerization is still not complete at the beginning of the nineties. The logical problems of 'concrete sciences' were already being discussed in the emerging 'philosophy of science' but, on the whole, the science of logic still remained behind the purview of the archaeologists of that period. Everybody who looks at the secondary school textbooks of the middle of this century and the scanty literature aimed at the general public of the same period will probably agree that archaeologists of that time could hardly achieve more: their own typology did not seem so bad in comparison with what they could learn about other scientific disciplines.

What has just been written about the natural sciences is almost entirely true about history and ethnography as well. There was not too much inspiration that could lead archaeologists to a position different from that which they were taking: let us note that Kossinna's starting point was, in addition to philology, just a kind of history, and that the cultural historical school was believed to represent ethnography. History at that time was primarily political history (hardly applicable to archaeology) and ethnography of that period also dealt with problems which could not be easily compared to the problems resulting from material remains. It is interesting to note, however, that the remarkable achievements of linguistic theory, known as linguistic structuralism, which spread widely in the period between the two wars, left no imprint at all on archaeology despite the fact that there was much to apply (cf. J. V. Neustupný 1958). Its impact on archaeology came much later and was mediated by its application in ethnography (Hodder 1982).

The typological paradigm also had psychological roots. Certain kinds of life experience of archaeologists had such a strong impact on their psychology that they could not help explaining them as universal models of human behaviour. Thus, some British archaeologists explained certain changes in the 'megalithic' ideology by the advent of missionaries, and for others the supposed cultural lag of Europe in comparison with the Near East formed an analogy to the relation between Victorian Britain and its colonies. The Scandinavians, whose modern history passed without any upheavals, had a tendency to explain prehistory by means of consecutive evolutionary steps. In contrast to this viewpoint Central European prehistory seemed to be full of wars, invasions, population movements, etc.; hardly any continuity in the historical process has been assumed.

Ideological motifs for sustaining the typological paradigm are very pronounced. This is obvious not only from the preferred questions and solutions but also from the problems that were ignored or underestimated. Let us name at least a few of them: the function of artifacts, economy and social organization. If such questions were posed at all, it was, for example, to use the social organization of the Germanic tribes as another attribute to differentiate them from other ethnic groups. The lists of diffused traits often contained ornamental motifs on pottery, next to the plough and the organization of the society; they were all put on the same level of importance in the 'historical' process (i.e. 'historical' in the sense of the Vienna school which often described itelf as the historical school).

2.2.3   *The crisis of the typologial paradigm*

The typological paradigm (or paradigms) was applied in archaeology without any serious difficulties until the middle of the twentieth century. This is not to say that there were no new ideas which would stand close to our 'modern' views; in fact, it would be surprising if there were none. When they appeared, however, they were not accepted as standards.

The first fifteen years (the second half of the 1940s and the 1950s) can be preliminarily characterized as a period when much new appeared without the archaeologists realizing it. The sixties witnessed a 'revolution' which meant that the changes taking place in archaeology could no longer go unnoticed. The new directions began to separate from the traditional performance of archaeology, and this process was often accompanied with great pride. It seemed to many that the revolution would demolish the wrecked old archaeology completely and would build something entirely new. Such a situation is typical of any new paradigm in any branch of human knowledge; it is also characteristic that most practitioners of archaeology went on along the old routes at the time when the first prophets had already announced the revolution. The situation has much progressed since the pioneering works of the first New Archaeologists but maxims of the new paradigm are still difficult to formulate.

The persuasion of the pioneers of the new paradigm that they are building something entirely new is no tactical manœuvre. Work is done in terms of contrasts; a question frequently discussed within the old framework becomes automatically a candidate for exclusion from the new paradigm. This was, for example, the fate of the Indoeuropean problem within Old World archaeology (cf. Renfrew 1987). So there is a real discontinuity in many respects.

A new paradigm takes its origin when the old one gets into

a crisis; this is brought about (1) by new questions (which the old paradigm is unable to answer), (2) by new theoretical and methodological principles and (3) by new facts which the old theoretical thinking is unable to explain. At the beginning there is a tendency to adjust the old theory by incorporating some of the new demands and by ignoring the unfitting facts. Ever more scientists realize that the old intellectual framework is untenable; they start building a new one or, which is typical of the young generation, they revolt and require an immediate change. The old paradigm does not die because somebody would disprove it by means of logical argument but simply because there remains nobody willing to defend it. This is the reason why it is so difficult to identify the moment when the new paradigm begins.

There are scientists who believe that everything is replaced, not a stone is left standing. Such a view is not only inconsistent with the epistemologial theory, it is also contradictory in respect of ascertained facts. The old paradigm is overcome dialectically, i.e. many of its positive aspects are retained: its continuity with the old theory is undeniable.

It must be pointed out that a new paradigm comes into being because the situation in human society and its scientific consciousness becomes ripe for it. The necessary conditions, however, typically appear in many parts of the world in the same historical period. It can hardly be assumed that the New Archaeology is born in one or two regions of the world and that it subsequently spreads to the other parts. But it happens that the evolution of human thought is faster in one region, which then 'influences' scientists in other countries who feel the need for changes but are not yet able to formulate the means by which to achieve them. Paradoxically, even archaeologists who strongly oppose diffusionism in their discipline are prone to believe that archaeological ideas appear as a result of diffusion from a modern centre. But let us return to more concrete questions of the new paradigm being born.

The end of World War II brought new ways of thinking almost everywhere among the nations practising archaeology. At the same time it resulted in a new configuration of social forces. The new historical situation revealed the role of economics and of social progress so markedly that no social science could ignore it any more. Now, history could not be explained as a result of the interplay of moral principles or as a consequence of erratic acts by individuals, as a fight of racial or ethnic groups, or as a random combination of independent formal factors. It became obvious that many things of the past cannot be understood without the knowledge of economics and the principles on which social systems work.

Many archaeologists sought to elucidate the economic and social order of prehistoric societies; they found that the typological paradigm had no answer. Moreover, it was not clear how it could bear on the questions. It was obvious that different types of artifacts do not reflect different social groups, that economics can hardly be influenced by the diffusion of personal ornaments, and that the so-called typological series as reconstructed by archaeology do not correspond either to effective changes of tools or to the evolution of social systems. Many archaeologists realized that much information on economics is contained in what we nowadays term ecofacts (mostly held in contempt by typologists) and/or in higher entities of the archaeological record such as the present-day components or settlement areas, which were of no interest to the practitioners of traditional archaeology. Not even graves can bear on ancient social order if they are looked upon exclusively as assemblages of types used for chronological ordering.

World War II was followed by an unprecedented development of the natural sciences and technological disciplines. Mathematics became accessible to many non-mathematicians who discovered its usefulness for concrete sciences. A lot of authors studied epistemological and logical problems of science, raising interest in these questions among archaeologists. All this has contributed to the creation of the necessary conditions for the emergence of a new paradigm. Examples of how the natural sciences and mathematics began 'helping' archaeology are well known. Not only did they become well prepared for the task but many of their methods became accessible now because the advent of modern technology alleviated the previous high cost of such analyses.

The first incursion of logics (or more exactly the philosophy of science) into archaeology was extremely important mainly because it stressed the role of deduction partly destroying the empirically orientated methodology borrowed from the natural sciences of the nineteenth century. It is not important in this connection that many of the New Archaeologists went to the other extreme position (denouncing induction completely); yet, this was the first conscious use of the results of general scientific methodology in archaeology. The issue is also interesting from the point of view of what we stated about the international character of the 'new' paradigm. At about the time when our American colleagues were applying Hempel's philosophy of science to archaeology, I was using another kind of epistemology based mainly on dialectics (Neustupný 1964, 1967; the main theses expressed in these publications are developed in this book).

The first large-scale applications of natural scientific methods to archaeology sometimes resulted from the initiative of the natural scientists while the traditional archaeologists remained neutral: they just did not feel to be in need of them. It is rarely realized that this was the case, for example, with the radiocarbon dating method in Europe. The situation changed somewhat when the results of the method proved that many cultural items previously believed to have diffused to Europe from the Near East could not have done so, for chronological reasons (Neustupný 1968, 1969); the same proved true in other parts of the Old World (Renfrew 1969). Something was wrong with the basic diffusionist assumptions. At the same time it became clear – also on the basis of radiocarbon dating – that the neolithic and eneolithic periods in Europe were much longer than had been previously assumed on the basis of traditional methodology. Moreover, the individual cultural groups of that period followed each other when found in the same territory. This made it likely that the groups (or 'cultures') were in fact developments of a single culture and did not represent various nations as suggested by Kossinna and his followers. These two cases are exactly the kinds of new facts that help undermine old paradigms according to Kuhn's theory.

It was, of course, not only the new facts brought by scientific methods that made the old paradigm less probable. Even the results of traditional research did not favour it. It was, for

example, a common assumption of many typological archaeologists that where two distinct archaeological groups were
found in a region (and, consequently, were believed to represent two ethnic groups) one had arrived from some distant
area. This was in fact a very important assumption as it would
be difficult to suggest a migration without the possibility of
pointing to the region of origin of the group arriving from
outside. The traditional archaeologists did not bother, of
course, to find any concrete area of origin for the particular
groups. At the beginning of the twentieth century there were
still large tracts of Europe which were archaeologically so little
known that they could be made responsible for the origin of
any culture. A typical suggestion was 'the steppes of southern
Russia' and the like. In the meantime, however, traditional
archaeological research has accumulated so much knowledge
on those previously poorly known regions that it has become
increasingly difficult (and now materially impossible) to
assume the origin of any prehistoric culture in any part of
Europe by mere speculation. This fact substantially limits
manœuvring within the old paradigm.

What may be even more significant is the fact that the
traditional typological paradigm was unable to answer a
number of questions formulated as early as the beginning of
this century. The Indoeuropean problem has not been solved
within the paradigm (cf. Renfrew 1987), the origin of many
archaeological groups has remained as obscure as before, and
even the relative chronology of prehistoric groups in Central
Europe has not substantially changed during the decades of
the typological paradigm. The number of finds has grown
enormously but the growth of our understanding of the past
has not followed. There was some progress in certain neglected periods and areas such as the mesolithic or the Middle
Ages but, on the whole, new ideas only emerged with the
advent of the elements of the new paradigm (newly formulated questions, the use of radiocarbon, seriation, etc.).

2.2.4   The new paradigm

It seems at first glance that the typologial paradigm is
not so wicked: the typological method itself is certainly a

useful procedure, the search for the origin of ethnic groups is no doubt legitimate, and even replies to the basic problem (the explanation of the variability of the archaeological record) are not lacking in sense. True, archaeology asks more questions these days, but is it not sufficient to supplement the traditional (typological) approach by these new questions? I believe that mere improvement is not enough, and the following chapters should point in this direction.

It might appear that I shall now describe the new paradigm which is to replace typology. It has already been observed that this is not yet possible as, despite the claims of some archaeologists, it does not yet seem that the new paradigm can be anything like developed, and originating paradigms cannot be formulated. This volume should help in the process of elucidating some problems of what I consider constitutes the new paradigm. It concentrates, however, on methodology and leaves theory more or less aside.

3

Genesis of the archaeological record

It is obvious to any layman who has ever visited archaeological excavations that there is a substantial difference
between what archaeologists discover and what life was like
at the place of the excavations in prehistoric or historic times.
Only a trained archaeologist with a firmly established paradigm can overlook this difference, mistaking the finds for the
real (though past and now long extinguished) living human
society. The period of implied identification of the two ways
of conceptualizing the past, i.e. the identification of the living
and the dead cultures, now seems to be over but only a
generation ago it was still commonplace.

Most archaeologists were prepared to acknowledge the
existence of the issue but they had good reasons for concen-
trating their attention exclusively on their records. Some
believed that when their finds were properly studied, they
would begin speaking, but that during the period of analysis
it would be premature to attempt more than to describe and to
analyse the materials. Others boldly declared that they would
never be able to say anything substantial about life as it was
lived by prehistoric peoples; the finds were the only remnants
of the past and, consequently, the only objects available for
their study. The former attitude is clearly less intelligent and
less defensible but most archaeologists of past generations,
when pressed for a statement, would probably have taken
that standpoint. The latter position may seem to be much
more deplorable to a present-day optimistic archaeologist but
it leads, by way of negation, to a more realistic perspective.

3.1 Living culture and dead culture

A living human society is a very complex system indeed. It operates by means of its culture, which is a structured set of extrasomatic means aimed at reproducing itself. To respond to this purpose, human culture has to reach into three principal spheres of life: (1) the intercourse between men and nature (often called *economics*), (2) that between men and men (often called *social relations*), and (3) the intercourse between men and their consciousness (sometimes called *ideology*). 'Cultural; is almost identical with 'human', or it has been so at least for the last 30 thousand years, when there is every ground to believe that even such simple 'natural' functions as eating and sleeping have had cultural forms.

Living culture is usually believed to consist of material and spiritual phenomena (or material and spiritual culture) but this bipartition may be a product of the point of view of our modern society with its sharp demarcation between physical labour and creative arts and science. The distinction between spiritual and material culture becomes very unclear once we leave our own times and this part of the world. Do upper palaeolithic female figurines belong to the material culture because they survived and the songs possibly sung during their manufacture to the spiritual culture because they did not? Or do the figurines represent spiritual culture because they are objects of art? What difference would there then be between the figurines and richly decorated (or undecorated) neolithic pots? Although possibly valid in our own society, the opposition of material to spiritual aspects of culture does not seem to fit all periods of human history. Such an opposition has in any case nothing to do with the question of what survives from the past.

We have first-hand knowledge of our own living culture, and it is often easy to obtain information on some aspects of the living culture of those peoples whose technological level, reached during the last three centuries, may be comparable to that supposed for some periods of European prehistory. A consideration of these cases makes it immediately obvious that any living culture is richer (usually much richer) than what survives in comparable archaeological contexts. This fact struck archaeologists long ago: they realized that their archaeological culture was dead culture. Archaeologists, however, do not seem to have drawn the analogy with nature far enough; in consequence of this they tacitly assumed that the 'dead' or archaeological culture was just a kind of less-rich living culture in which many items had not been preserved. The concept of 'material culture' certainly played a role in this incorrect assumption: if material culture consists of material objects, then it is clear that many of these objects do survive in such a state that they can be directly compared to living objects.

The German archaeologist H. J. Eggers clearly saw some of the differences between living and dead cultures as early as the fifties (cf. Eggers 1959, 225–76). According to him the archaeological record has been reduced both qualitatively and quantitatively in relation to the living culture of which it is a selection; it therefore does not allow the same questions to be posed as the written record does. Eggers still considered the dead culture to be more or less a subset of items selected from the living culture.

A system of stimulating ideas on these issues was formulated by Michael Schiffer in the seventies (Schiffer 1972, 1976). He argued that archaeological remains had gone through a series of processes, cultural and non-cultural, which had transformed them spatially, quantitatively, formally and relationally. Archaeological data were totally silent; the only way to relate them to 'behavioural variables' was through statements testable in an ongoing system. Schiffer coined the term 'correlates' for such statements, while his 'transforms' denoted a similar concept relating archaeological variables as outputs of a once-living system to the variables of that system. When using correlates and transforms one has to turn to 'additional but necessary bits of information' which Schiffer terms stipulations. Correlates and transforms are generated by a process 'not unlike the way a child learns the grammar of a language', i.e. more or less unconsciously.

This seems to be the main point of my disagreement with Schiffer. A child can learn grammar because those who teach him know it, but there is nobody to teach us prehistoric life.

Schiffer's attitude in this respect is equivalent to saying that his correlates and transforms can somehow be derived from the archaeological record; it is my conviction that they cannot. The next pages demonstrate that the difference between living and dead archaeological culture reaches much deeper than is usually believed.

3.2   The concept of transformation

Once it ceases to fulfil its function, human culture dies and changes into the archaeologial record. Its 'death', however, is only the first step in the many transformations that change its very substance. The transformations of cultural items, be it whole cultures or single facts (i.e. either artifacts or ecofacts) is a never-ending process: not even the deposition of finds in a museum brings the changes to an end.

Inorganic nature, when left alone, tends towards an unorganized state. The relative lack or decrease of organization is called *entropy* which, being the opposite of information, can be measured by means of information theory concepts. The higher the probability that an artifact has originated through forces of nature, the less information it contains, and the higher the measure of entropy. On the other hand entropy decreases when the probability of an object's being conditioned or intentionally formed by man increases. The consideration of the probability of a pebble tool occurring as a consequence of natural factors has always been one of the common methods of judging its intentionality even by those archaeologists who were not acquainted with the concept of entropy.

The manufacture of artifacts is connected with a decrease in the measure of entropy and an increase in the measure of information. The same applies to most ecofacts and, of course, to all the higher levels of artifactual entities. When artifacts leave the sphere of living culture, for example by being discarded, they return to the sphere of natural (physical) objects: they lose any function, meaning or significance, and their formal and spatial organization disintegrates. Consequently, the information they carry decreases and entropy grows. The process is irreversible: the information lost can never be retrieved from the disintegrated artifacts themselves as it is just not there any more. This clearly follows from the basic theses of information theory.

In the preceding paragraphs I have tried to suggest that the transformation of artifacts and ecofacts caused by their transition into dead (archaeological) culture is more than a selection of certain parts of the 'complete' living culture. It is a process of information loss or, to put it in other words, the return of artifacts and ecofacts into nature from which they were isolated by man, formed according to his will, and/or moved to an 'unnatural' place during their use. This growth in entropy is more or less a natural process as man, if he is involved at all, acts here as a natural destroying force; it has been only in the last century or so that archaeologists have tried to slow down the destruction by means of conservation techniques applied to finds, and protection measures applied to sites.

At the same time it has become clear that certain classes of information, and among them very important ones, are completely and irrevocably lost: they cannot be wrought out of finds for the simple reason that they did not survive. It is especially the loss of facts from the living sphere that can never be reversed.

The word 'transformation' is more or less synonymous with 'change' in everyday speech. I shall usually reserve the term for the changes that artifacts and ecofacts undergo in the course of, and following, their exit from the living culture. During their existence as physical objects, artifacts pass from the phase of formation (usually manufacture or mass production) to the phase of use and ultimately to transformations. Formation and use clearly belong to the sphere of living culture. The first phase in the life of an artifact, formation, produces information and reduces entropy. The second phase, use, contains opposite tendencies, since an artifact is changed by use: one could argue that entropy is already increasing in this phase. This change, however, is insignificant in comparison with the transformations that follow.

3.3   The classes of transformations

The number and the variety of changes that affect the living culture and later the dead, already transformed, culture are great. First of all there is a transformation which turns the living culture into the archaeological record (i.e. the dead culture). In the light of subsequent changes, it is not so much important what the transforming agent was – whether man or nature; it is the effect on the kind of organization or order contained in the archaeological facts that is vital. From this point of view there are two major groups of transformations: spatial and formal. Both of them can be either qualitative or quantitative. They can work at the same time or in sequence.

3.3.1   Exit transformation

Exit transformation operates on the living culture. It is the process that ends the life of a fact (i.e. an artifact or an ecofact); from another perspective it can be considered as the moment or the period of time which divides the two kinds of culture. On the side of the living system there are usually some changes such as wear, fragmentation, deposition into a special environment, etc.; on the side of the dead culture there are things that have no observable function, meaning and/or significance any more. By going through the exit transformation, artifacts and ecofacts leave the sphere of dynamic cultural systems and become part of static archaeological systems if there are any dynamics in the archaeological record, they are the dynamics of the surrounding nature, a fact that invariably leads to further loss of information. The artifacts and ecofacts are separated from their human agent who made them act and, in consequence of this separation, they lose cultural time, in which function, meaning and significance operate. From that point onwards, they are subject to cosmic time, as their constituents were before being selected and formed by man. The period of exit is usually quite short but occasionally it may last up to several centuries, especially in the case of things that are kept above ground and that serve, or can serve, their original purpose from time to time. This is often the case with jewels or royal insignia before they turn into symbols and subsequently into museum objects.

The moment of death can be determined fairly accurately with animals and plants on the basis of the observation of certain life functions, but it may not be as simple with artifacts, which need not change their outer appearance during their exit. Some prehistoric tools and ornaments (especially stone tools and golden ornaments) often display no change at all and could be used again in modern times; this seems to be one of the reasons why many archaeologists have mistaken archaeological objects for living artifacts.

The exit transformation may be caused by a variety of processes. Both artifacts and ecofacts may leave the living culture because of being damaged or destroyed and, consequently, discarded or deserted, because of being needed no more (e.g. a house in a deserted village), because of becoming inaccessible as a result of some natural event (sites covered by flood deposits, sunken ships), because of their intentional deposition and closure for ritual reasons (e.g. offerings in bogs, contents of graves), because of being forgotten (hoards) or lost. The consumption of food and fuel is also among the causes of exit. Despite the fact that the exit of an artifact or ecofact need not be accompanied by either a formal or a spatial change, it frequently happens to be so. Pottery has most often gone past the point of exit because it disintegrated into sherds, stone tools because their edges turned blunt. Many artifacts, untransformed from the point of view of their shape, were deposited in graves and in this way sealed from their living contemporaries.

It is often believed that the domain of archaeological concern can be defined as 'things excavated from the earth' but the earth cover is clearly a secondary phenomenon which does not unmistakably separate the dead from the living culture. Animal bones in prehistoric sites may serve as an example. It should be pointed out that it is not the death of animals that marks the point of exit for the 'archaeological' bones. The dead parts of animal bodies serving as food still belong to the living culture. When the bones have been used up and discarded by humans but are serving as food for their dogs, they can still be regarded as a part of the living culture. It is only when nobody cares any more that the point of exit is reached. This, however, does not mean that the bones would automatically be immediately buried under the earth: they may lie on the surface for many years so that most of them disintegrate completely; the rest get under the surface and may be subject to further decomposition there. We could argue that in typical archaeological situations in Central Europe less than 5 per cent of animal bones get into the earth and survive. In fact, it may be much less.

3.3.2 Spatial transformations

As Albert Spaulding pointed out years ago (1960), there are only two dimensions that archaeologists can observe in the case of a dead (archaeological) culture: space and form. Space transformations move artifacts and ecofacts (and their parts) to a place different from that they occupied within the living culture and/or different from the result of a previous transformation.

At least one of the frequent spatial transformations takes place within the living culture: the removal of rubbish to a special area used for its deposition. In fact the people who dispose of the refuse act similarly to those modern people who remove cultural layers of a prehistoric site because they need to use the area. Such behaviour is not directed towards parts of a formerly living culture as much as towards present-day needs. However, if the disposal of rubbish were subject to some ritual, it would become a full part of the living culture and possible transformations would start only later.

Many archaeologists believe that it is important to investigate whether particular spatial transformations have been caused by man or nature. This may not be always interesting in view of the fact that ancient or modern people who transferred archaeological records to another place (by building or destroying mounds, ramparts, settlement sites, etc.) acted as blind natural forces. The only possible exception to this is what I describe as the archaeological transformation *sensu stricto*, i.e. the removal of archaeological finds from their natural and cultural environment and their transportation to some kind of collection (this need not be museum collections as laymen who plunder archaeological sites also clearly belong to this category). The human actor, who behaves intentionally in this case, is of importance.

Many examples of spatial transformations of the archaeological record are well known. The silting of deserted underground features by the cultural layer previously accumulated in their surroundings is responsible for the replacement of very many artifacts, bones, plant remains, etc. contained in that layer. The contents of graves can be put in partial or complete disorder both by burrowing animals and by grave robbers (some of them prehistoric) and removed to a distance of many kilometres by modern building machines and trucks.

Artifacts are rarely found at exactly the place where they were deposited by their users, i.e. without any transformation. Yet most graves, if undisturbed, belong to this non-transformed or little transformed category, and some hoards, if excavated by archaeologists, also reveal their original spatial structure. Sometimes, as an exception, we are lucky enough to discover a prehistoric house with everything in its original position; Pompeii, although not prehistoric in date, may be the very best and the most extensive example. In the majority of prehistoric sites, however, fragments of pottery, tools and animal bones are mixed in the so-called cultural layer, which often does not survive other than in the fill of subterranean cavities: this is often the tertiary deposition of facts (the minimum sequence would be: on the surface → in the cultural layer → in the cavity).

The important difference between archaeological facts undisplaced by spatial transformations on the one hand and those displaced (possibly several times) on the other has been recognized already within traditional methodology (J. V. Neustupný 1958). The former case has been described as intentional assemblages, the latter unintentional. It has been argued that it is only in the intentional assemblages that the 'associated' facts can be considered to be connected by chronological and functional links, because things in unintentional deposits can be mixed mechanically and their association need not reflect any common destination or purpose. In fact, archaeologists who worked within the traditional migrationist paradigm often 'proved' contemporaneity of cultures by means of the common occurrence of their types in spatially transformed deposits; using this methodology it is easy to prove contemporaneity of any pair of artifact types.

3.3.3   Formal transformations

Some artifacts and ecofacts leave the living culture because of the destruction that took place through their use. This kind of exit is typical for pottery but, as noted earlier, it is by no means universal. Many cultural items are destroyed formally only after reaching the point of exit.

The destructive transformation changes archaeological facts through material decay and/or mechanical destruction. The object of decay is the matter of which facts consist. It is well known that organic substances do not survive in most archaeological contexts throughout the world, and many archaeologists still believe that it is in fact the deficiency of wooden objects, leather, textiles, etc. that distinguishes the living from the dead culture. In some environments, however, such as peat bogs or arid deserts, organic material conserves quite well, without changing anything of principle. Moreover, facts whose main constituents are easily perishable substances survive from time to time almost anywhere, so that they are retrievable at least as rare examples.

It is widely held that stone implements, sherds of fired clay and bones are almost immortal. This is possibly true of hard stone – unless it gets into a rapid stream whose bed it shares with other stones. There is no question that bones disintegrate easily, and the same is also true of prehistoric pottery. Some archaeologists believe that those fragments of vessels that are missing in one part of the cultural layer would be found in the surrounding areas if these were properly excavated. My experience from extensive excavations of bronze age sites in Bohemia shows that excavating the neighbouring areas brings to light only sherds of new pots, whose major parts are again missing. The supposition that one could restore whole vessels by excavating a whole site simply does not work.

Mechanical forces such as the trampling down of objects

lying near the surface of a cultural layer, or physical factors such as rapid changes of water content and temperature, usually affect the shape of facts. They break into pieces in such a way that the whole may be unrecognizable. Some kinds of modern destruction, such as sand digging, are complex: everything is destroyed completely. In the best case archaeological artifacts may remain embedded in a concrete wall at a distance of many miles from the original site.

The archaeological transformation *sensu stricto* must be mentioned again. Even if the process of excavation is very careful and the whole cultural layer is water sieved, archaeologists still miss fragments of facts whose diameter is less than the sieve meshes used. Theoretically, at least, important information is lost in this way (pollen grains, etc.).

Thus, both spatial and formal transformations imply a destructuring of the archaeological record. The formal transformations annihilate or seriously impair the structure of both individual facts and their sets; the space transformation affects mainly sets of facts, demolishing the original network of their interrelationships that reflected the functioning of the living culture. Although the destruction is sometimes annihilation, at least something survives in many instances.

3.4   Quantitative aspects of transformations

For many decades archaeologists showed very little interest in the quantitative aspects of their records; later there came a period of measuring and counting everything. The results, especially in the case of counting, frequently proved to be unsatisfactory. The reason for this may be found in the problems discussed in the following paragraphs.

It is sometimes believed that the quantitative relations observed in the archaeological record reflect relations in the living culture more or less directly. It is often found in the archaeological literature that people of culture A used very many ceramic bowls because their settlement sites produce bowl fragments in large quantities. The number of pigs approximately equalled the number of cattle because the bone counts of the two species are the same or because the minimum number of individuals does not differ. When the percentage of the pottery decorated with incisions does not change in two consecutive phases, it clearly means that the incisions were invariant with time. A culture group whose number of sites makes one quarter of the total for another culture group in the same territory had a very low population density indeed. If one pollen spectrum, connected with a grave, has only one half of the number of oak pollen grains found in another one (connected with a later grave), this is a clear indication that oak woods grew at the expense of other biotopes. All these statements can be shown to be invalid; it is only by chance if they happen to be true.

There are certain quantities in the archaeological record that are only slightly affected by any kind of transformation; these can be termed *absolute quantities*. They include, for example, the length of well-preserved artifacts or the distance between sites, possibly the number of graves in a completely excavated cemetery etc. The age of death of human skeletons and their body height, both derived from diagnostic properties of bones and from a model of living human populations, are also absolute numbers or intervals on an absolute scale. Transformations do affect them but it is only the probability of measuring the right value that changes; the values themselves are not appreciably transformed. Typically, absolute quantities are measured in physical units such as metres, years, etc. When it comes to counts, however, everything changes: most counts are heavily affected by transformations such as fragmentation, cumulation, reduction and the loss of evidence for the rate of change.

3.4.1 Fragmentation

Disintegration into pieces or fragmentation are partly qualitative problems. As such, however, they can be easily overcome in most instances: it is frequently possible to reconstruct the whole artifact even from a very small fragment. The situation is more complicated with the quantitative aspect. As in the case of pottery, for example, the number of pieces into which a pot breaks depends on too many factors. No doubt, the number of fragments averages out at a fixed value for a particular type of vessel, but this average, as shown by the study of pottery finds, is useful only in the case of very large samples. As a result, it is impossible to reconstruct the original number of vessels on the basis of the number of sherds, not even on the unrealistic assumption that nothing has decayed completely.

Of course, fragments are ugly in museum exhibitions, but this is not the main reason why archaeologists dislike them: if it were known how many vessels and how many other artifacts there were per house in a village, it could lead to a deeper insight into the life of the prehistoric (or historic) community. The problem of fragmentation turns this into a difficult question. Some archaeologists try to overcome this difficulty by counting something like a 'minimum number of vessels' (based, perhaps, on the number of rim sherds that clearly belong to different pieces of pottery); this may work in the case of small complexes but it is often impossible to use this method for huge samples with hundreds or thousands of pots.

It is good luck that not everything in the archaeological record is found broken into pieces. Let us recall at least two important examples: graves and houses. Most other immobile entities and many (but not all) artifacts found in graves also turn out as wholes. Settlement sites, however, sometimes resemble strewn fragments if there are what appear to be satellite sites (homesteads) dispersed over a considerable area: one feels that certain subsets of the homesteads may have formed a whole (something like a village) but it is impossible to say how many of them and which.

3.4.2   Cumulation

Let us assume that the problem of fragmentation has been overcome. What we have to face next is the cumulative property of archaeological artifacts and ecofacts. When 500 house ruins are found in a neolithic village which lasted for some 600 years, everyone will agree that all the houses could not have functioned at the same time. Surprisingly, some archaeologists who excavate thirty house plans from one archaeological phase readily accept that most, if not all of them, formed a village at one time in prehistory. This could only be true if the duration of the phase equalled the mean life of a house, which is rarely the case. The houses usually last for less than one distinguishable archaeological phase and, consequently, they cannot all be contemporaneous: their remnants accumulate at the site, and so, in fact, do all the other kinds of artifacts and ecofacts.

Any fact of a living culture has a mean lifetime which expresses the average number of years elapsed between the production and the exit of specimens of the class to which the fact belongs. A particular vessel of type X may survive three times as long as other vessels of the same class (type), but this does not matter in our case as we are interested in sets of artifacts, not in individual pieces. It is the mean lifetime which determines how rapidly remains of a particular artifact or ecofact will accumulate at a site. The longer the lifetime, the fewer artifacts will be found. It can be shown that the following equation holds (on the condition of a more or less constant production rate):

$$R = Ht/z$$

where R means the number of facts accumulated during the period of t years, H means the average number of facts existing at any chosen moment of prehistory or history; their mean lifetime is z. For example a village consisting of four houses ($H = 4$) whose mean lifetime is ten years ($z = 10$) will produce forty house plans ($R = 40$) if the village remained at the same place for 100 years ($t = 100$). The condition is that the number of families (or, more exactly, the number of houses H) neither increased nor decreased during the period of t years. The equation can be solved for any of its variables. It is no accident that it resembles a similar equation known from demography: it describes the behaviour of a simple type of dynamic system (usually called stationary).

Each class of artifacts and ecofacts has its own mean lifetime, and this can be supposed to vary enormously. It may be something from several weeks to several years for prehistoric pottery, and from several years to several decades for a house. Prehistoric people themselves had a 'lifetime' (called life expectancy) between twenty and thirty years; for particular populations, however, it can be set much more exactly.

The effect of lifetimes can be seen from the following example. Let us assume that a prehistoric community used several types of vessels. One of them, the water-jar, permanently placed in the corner of a house, had a lifetime of ten years. Another one, a cup used for drinking, did not survive four months on the average. There was one cup to each jar in the living culture. Because of the great difference in the lifetimes, however, there will be thirty broken cups to each broken jar in the archaeological record. This is certainly an extreme example but less striking cases are common.

Lifetimes, of buildings for example, are often guessed at casually, but the numbers should be considered carefully; one has to bear in mind that by supposing a mean lifetime of some twenty years instead of, say, seven years for a neolithic house, one in fact suggests three times as many people in the neolithic village.

The lifetimes, of course, cannot be observed by archaeologists but their impact upon the solution of almost any archaeological problem is so great that we should try to say at least something about them. Archaeologists are not always confined to guesses or modern analogies. If we can start from a well-known lifetime (such as the life expectancy of prehistoric populations) we can sometimes derive other lifetimes by simple calculations. Let us use the following symbols: P^0 for the population inhabiting one house (usually one family), e_0 for the life expectancy at birth and D for the number of deaths occurring in population P. We get

$$D^0 = P^0 t / e_0,$$

If there were H houses to one village, the number of deaths in the village would be

$$D' = H P^0 t / e_0$$

H and t are here the same as in the preceding paragraphs, so we get

$$R = Ht/z \text{ and}$$

$$Ht = Rz$$

Substituting, we have

$$D' = P^0Rz/e_0 \text{ and}$$

$$z = D'e_0/P^0R$$

where the variables on the right side can be either observed archaeologically (D' and R) or calculated using well-defined demographic formulas (for e_0 and P^0). The equation can be simplified to remove its dependence on the unknown number of small children. When there is a completely excavated cemetery and a completely excavated settlement site of the same population group, the lifetime of a house can be calculated with an acceptable accuracy. It is, of course, very difficult to obtain such a set of data and, in fact, I do not know of any.

3.4.3 Reduction

So far we have tacitly supposed that at least something survives from each artifact and ecofact. This is clearly an unrealistic assumption: there is no doubt that some facts are completely annihilated in the course of post-exit transformations. If a class of objects, e.g. textiles, disappears as a whole, it is surprisingly a lesser cause of methodological difficulties than if it is destroyed only partially. The reason for this is that in the former case nobody doubts the lack of the record but in the latter case the disappearance of evidence is often subject to an argument: archaeologists tend to take the reduced number of facts at its face value, i.e. as equal to the actual number of facts in the living culture. The quantitative *reduction* of the archaeological record is, however, tremendous. This may not be very obvious to a field archaeologist who counts the number of finds in baskets or boxes and compares it with his previous experience.

It is well known that some kinds of evidence such as fields, roads, objects made of perishable substances, food, etc. are rarely found in many parts of the world but stone artifacts, pottery and bones (to name a few examples) are extremely frequent. Yet even the amount of these 'frequent' finds is greatly reduced: we could argue in another connection that what survives of prehistoric pottery and bones is probably less than 5 per cent of the original total in many instances. This becomes clear from the comparison of the total number of bones with the 'minimum number of individuals' (MNI) found in small and medium-sized excavations: there are typially some five bones per individual (MNI) while a fully grown domestic animal has some 240 bones. This, however, does not mean that five bones survive from each animal: there must be very many instances of individuals from whom nothing at all remains. (Note. The ratio between the bone count and the MNI becomes higher in complexes of roughly 1000 bones and more; this is clearly a consequence of the underestimation of the MNI in large collections of bones.)

The effect of the reduction process upon the archaeological record is made even worse by the fact that this process is selective: it does not reduce the same category of artifacts or ecofacts to the same degree. To use the example of animal bones again: it can be proved that small bones are significantly underrepresented in relation to big bones. This, of course, favours big species (such as *Bos*) and adult individuals of all species. Smaller and younger animals would occur in the archaeological record in lesser quantities – both absolutely and relatively.

The causes of reduction are manifold. Fragmentation and further crushing of fragments seems to be the basis as fragments usually conserve much worse than whole objects. The main factor responsible for the total disappearance of archaeological remains, however, seems to be climatic (rapid changes of moisture and temperature), bacterial and vegetational (in the case of organic substances) and chemical (mainly oxidation of items lying on the surface and the ionizing effect of chemicals contained in the soil). On the whole, however, the most dangerous placement for any archaeological fact is on the surface; those parts of the record that get quickly into the soil have a much greater probability of survival. This seems to be a general rule despite the fact that soil acids are responsible for the almost complete dissolution of bones in many sites.

The archaeological transformation *sensu stricto* should not be forgotten. It is well known how archaeologists of the last century (and, I am told, some of the end of the twentieth century as well) reduced their record by throwing away many finds which they considered uninformative. In this way handaxes were stripped of the flakes that accompanied them, animal bones were discarded, the position of vessels and tools in graves went unnoticed, etc. As any archaeological excavation is a selection from an endless set of potentially observable information, it would be naïve to assume that present-day archaeologists have the privilege of picking up everything of importance. No archaeologist can excavate without reducing his record in a drastic way. Lewis Binford has called for excavations as a means of testing hypotheses and his position has been attacked as arrogant in respect of the archaeological record. However, if the Binfordian strategy is followed with a non-radical interpretation, excavations can produce data important at least in one respect. Otherwise, in the case of 'general' excavations aimed at discovering *something*, the result may be even worse because 'careful' fieldwork is often fieldwork directed by the old paradigm.

It is not only by throwing away their data that archaeologists influence their records. We could argue, for example, that the frequency of eneolithic sites in Bohemia reflects, in inverse order, the proportion of decorated pottery. This phenomenon, with analogies in many countries and many periods of archaeological concern, reflects both the attitude of laymen, who usually report on the discovery of new sites, and the attitude of archaeologists, who may not be attracted by the undecorated plain pottery. The scarcity of chronologically sensitive attributes also plays its role.

What is most interesting for us in this context, however, is the quantitative effect of these reduction processes. Because of many local conditions, it is difficult if not impossible to guess the measure of reduction in specific instances. Not only is reduction selective in the sense outlined above, it is also largely unpredictable (with the exception of some trivial cases with either complete or zero reduction exemplified by wood and hard stone, respectively). This makes it impossible, at least at present, to attempt to judge the number of animals in prehistoric herds on the basis of the quantity of bones found in a site, or to derive the number of pots in a household from the count of vessel sherds uncovered in the cultural layer associated with a house. I hope that further research into the problems of reduction will prove that my views are too pessimistic, but nothing so far suggests that this is the case.

Fortunately, there are some classes of artifacts or other kinds of artifactual entities whose numbers, if obtained by large-scale careful excavations, may not be appreciably reduced. Where postholes are sufficiently deep to withstand intensive ploughing, a neolithic village such as flourished in Central Europe in the sixth millennium BC will survive with most of its house plans identifiable. The number of houses will not be reduced significantly in this case, and their great quantity is to be explained as a result of the cumulative transformation. Similarly, if graves are not shallow, a completely excavated prehistoric cemetery may yield the number of graves, of skeletons, of grave groups, of individual artifacts, etc. that have not been severely affected by the reduction process. On the other hand, cemeteries consisting of shallow graves, common in the *urnfield* period of the bronze age and the early iron age of Central Europe, can be substantially reduced after several years of intensive ploughing. The intermediate case, with some graves deep and some shallow, is again the most difficult to untangle. Some artifacts such as flint knives, stone axes, adzes, etc., if obtained during modern excavations (preferably with sieving of the cultural layer), can be considered as a fair approximation of the original (cumulative) numbers, unaffected by the reduction transformation. There are certainly more examples.

3.4.4   *Unknown growth rate*

Both the absolute and the relative numbers of items in groupings of archaeological facts change. Thus, taking into account the typological division of pottery, it is clear that the relative proportion of the types will not remain constant with time. The cause of the observed change was formerly attributed to changes of 'fashion', to 'influences' from neighbouring territories or to the fusion with other ethnic groups living in the same territory. It is widely held now that the predilection for some sorts of pottery shapes and decoration motifs could have been determined by the social sphere: the appearance and spread of highly decorated beakers in certain culture groups of eneolithic Europe (Corded Ware and Bell Beaker, i.e. third millennium BC) has been interpreted as a reflection

of the need for expressing social prestige in these communities (Shennan 1976). Not everything can be explained in this
way however: the changes are certainly partly due to the
function of artifacts, and other manifestations of variability
cannot be understood unless we assume the interference of
arbitrary processes. Be that as it may in specific instances, the
overall tendency to change remains a fact in any human
culture, and it affects any of its subsystems.

Archaeologists cannot observe the change itself (which is
one of the consequences of the exit transformation) but individual states of the 'evolutionary' process are amenable to
empirical knowledge. It is rare, however, to have access to
short-lived deposits which would allow not only the qualitative definition of types but also exact measurements of their
frequency. Archaeological deposits, e.g. the contents of
various pits or layers in settlement sites, usually cover long
periods and are therefore subject to cumulative transformation; it is difficult to separate the effect of cumulation
from the effect of the growth rate.

It is obvious that some kinds of artifacts and some kinds of
attributes become much more frequent during certain
archaeological phases, while others may disappear at the
same time. Such fluctuations in frequency can be expressed in
terms of the changing rate of growth, whether positive or
negative, and they can be approximated, for rather short
periods, by means of a stable model (in this connection
'stable' means 'with a stable growth rate'; it is a concept
different from stationarity or 'zero growth rate'). Conceptualizing the problem of growth by means of the stable dynamic
model, a very simple model, nevertheless produces quite
interesting results.

Table 3.1 shows an example of how an assemblage of four
types can behave, given certain values of the growth rate (r)
and certain values of the mean lifetime (z). The 'types' in this
table, which is a simulated example, can be visualized as
different forms of pottery. Form no. 1 has a yearly growth rate
of 1 per cent ($r = 0.01$; this means that the number of specimens of type 1 doubles every seventy years), and a mean
lifetime of three years. There are four vessels of this form in an
average household at the beginning ($H_0 = 4$), and this results

in some six to seven vessels after fifty years of settlement at the same site (H_{50} = 6.59). Because of the joint effect of both the rate of growth and the cumulative transformation, however, fragments of some eighty-six vessels of type 1 (i.e. R_{50} = 86.5) accumulate in the culture layer of an average household. The interesting consequences of this model for the calculation and the understanding of percentages will be discussed later.

It is important to realize that what archaeologists have at their disposal is neither H_0 nor H_{50}, both observable to pre-historic people; it is clearly the value of R_{50}, and this is quite unlike anything that could be observed from within living prehistoric cultures.

3.4.5   Counts and percentages

Archaeologists became aware of the quantitative bias in the archaeological record very early: the obvious way to overcome it was to replace the absolute numbers of facts by some relative numbers such as ratios between types of stone implements. A logical extension of this procedure, applicable to whole classes of types, is the calculation of percentages. Percentages are certainly the only expedient in very many cases and it is for this very reason that we should be aware of the many problems that their use implies.

The introduction of some sort of relative values instead of absolute counts is quite sensible: if there is a uniform rate of reduction for a whole class of types (e.g. for pottery types), the substitution of percentages for counts should solve many problems. In addition to reduction, however, fragmentation can also greatly influence the outcome: on finding 100 sherds from a single vessel of type A and ten sherds from several vessels of type B, the percentages calculated on the basis of sherd counts will not correspond to anything real. Fortu-nately there are some methods for transforming fragments back to individuals (such as the method of assessing the minimum number of individuals in archaeozoology, also applied to pottery), and this has been done successfully for many sites throughout the world.

Unfortunately, even removing the effect of fragmentation

and assuming a uniform rate of reduction for all the facts involved, there still remain serious problems. The main reason is that the two other transformations, i.e. cumulation and the unknown growth rate, also influence percentages.

In Table 3.1 the percentage of accumulated remains of type 1 is approximately 29 while the percentage of the same type in the living culture was clearly greater at all times. Type 4 (with a very low mean lifetime) never exceeded 14 per cent in the living culture but it reached 43 per cent of the total in the 'archaeological' culture. Most surprisingly, the absolute count of type 3 remained constant in the live culture (two vessels) but its percentage in periods 0 and 50 differed; the difference is not very pronounced in Table 3.1 but changing some of the parameters of the table only slightly could easily effect a much more pronounced difference (cf. Table 3.2 where the effect of the cumulative transformation has been negated by setting $z = 1$).

Some of those who firmly believe in percentages could possibly argue that the distortion would not be as bad as suggested by our tables, if the parameters of the transforming equations had smaller values. However, this is hardly possible to achieve as, according to what we know about the rate of change of archaeological attributes and types, the growth rate of ± 1 per cent is not exaggerated and the values for the lifetime of vessels between half a year and three years also seem to be quite realistic. It is only the time of growth and cumulation (t) that can possibly be reduced to give a smaller distortion. Thus, those who want to continue to use percentages as the level of observation should look for deposits which formed as quickly as possible. No doubt, they will soon come across the problem of random variability as short-term deposits usually do not contain a quantity of finds sufficient to make the differences between percentages statistically significant. We shall see later how to tackle this problem from another angle.

3.4.6   The research bias

The state of research may seriously influence quantitative aspects of the archaeological record. What is generally

Table 3.1. *Changes occurring in a simulated population of archaeological types after fifty years.* $H_t = H_0 e^{rt}$; $R_t = H_0(e^{rt} - 1)/rz$.

type	r	z	H_0	%	H_{50}	%	R_{50}	%
1	0.01	3	4	33.33	6.59	54.88	86.50	28.88
2	−0.02	2.5	5	41.67	1.84	15.22	63.21	21.11
3	0	5	2	16.67	2	16.55	20	6.68
4	0.01	0.5	1	8.33	1.65	13.65	129.74	43.33

Table 3.2. *Changes occurring in a simulated population of archaeological types after fifty years. The starting values of z is slightly changed in comparison with Table 3.1.*

type	r	z	H_0	%	H_{50}	%	R_{50}	%
1	0.02	1	4	33.33	10.87	66.44	343.66	51.55
2	−0.02	1	5	41.67	1.84	11.25	158.03	23.70
3	0	1	2	16.67	2	12.22	100.14	15.02
4	0.01	1	1	8.33	1.65	10.09	64.87	9.73

discussed in this context is the problem of the incompleteness of fieldwork, but the issue seems to be wider.

Archaeologists usually select a limited subset out of the total population of the 'data' which have survived all the preceding transformations. Their preferences are guided either by the frequency of the occurrence of a particular type of finds (frequent types are usually overrepresented in the record), or by some kind of paradigmatic bias. Thus, many archaeologists of the first half of this century did not collect animal bones, which did not seem to offer anything of importance for the solution of problems posed by the typological paradigm. For more or less the same reason (and, of course, also for reasons of economy), archaeologists in some countries threw away undecorated sherds and flint waste. When I worked for a rescue program in a coal mining district of Bohemia, I discovered almost exclusively settlement sites; graves occurred only rarely. One of my colleagues surprisingly found almost nothing except for a few graves. Either he or I had a preference which, of course, influenced the archaeological record of the region.

The problem of the effect of the research strategy on the quantitative aspect of archaeological finds is not a simple one. The main reason is that few people are able to overcome the restrictions on their thinking imposed by their paradigms. Moreover, most finds have been obtained by preceding generations of archaeologists, whose opinion on the importance of various kinds of field observations was different. Modern sampling strategies do help but they cannot remove those biases whose basis is paradigmatic.

3.5 The specific nature of the archaeological record

It is commonly held that the most important properties of the archaeological record are its material character and its incompleteness. This is not entirely misleading, as archaeological finds are indeed material things and very incomplete, but it does not fully explain the specificity of archaeology: many objects which play a principal role in 'written' history are also material. The steam engine is a historically important concept (an important historical source) but it is, undoubtedly, a material thing. Nuclear weapons are certainly not spiritual but they still cannot be ignored by historians. Some would argue that the material character of the archaeological record should be interpreted as 'exclusively material'. An argument to the contrary is that artifacts and their attributes were frequently signs, symbols, or images expressing ideas, so there is nothing purely or exclusively material in them.

As to the incompleteness supposed to distinguish the archaeological record, it seems to be equally typical of many other kinds of scientific data. In fact, any record of the past is incomplete. This is well known, for example, to historians whose research is concerned with the early Middle Ages of Europe: first, not many written sources are available in some regions and, second, those that have survived are not very informative, reflecting only some aspects of the life of the period. It would be naïve to believe that it is just that part of the archaeological record which we would like to have that has survived from the past.

Clearly, it is neither the formal nor the spatial transformations (whether in their qualitative or quantitative aspects) that determine the specific character of the archaeological record. They merely result in incompleteness and loss of information but it is a common feature of all sciences concerned with the past that such losses occur in their records. It seems, however, that the exit transformation is not fully matched in other historical disciplines. Exit separates the elements of the living culture from their living agents – ancient people – and turns them into static systems. In consequence, no direct information about the dynamic aspects of archaeological artifacts and ecofacts can be derived from the artifacts and ecofacts themselves. The 'dynamic aspects' include not only change and development but also function, meaning and significance of archaeological facts, concepts which have no sense outside the framework of passing time.

It is possible to maintain that written historical sources are no better in this respect. I am going to suggest, however, that this is not the case. Language is a highly refined tool for expressing any kind of dynamics: change, movement, development, function, meaning, significance, etc. Words are loaded with time; verbal statements need not be true but they do express life. In contrast to this, archaeological facts lack the time coordinate completely; theirs are only space and form. Time, of course, has left its imprint on everything in archaeology but only in the form of spatial or formal properties.

Written history is not the only sphere where the dynamics of life are present as a matter of fact. Ethnography of 'primitive' societies is another discipline of this kind; it is nowadays mostly confined to the study of texts (plus occasionally drawings, photographs and possibly museum exhibits). Any part of present-day life, including its theory, can become a source for the dynamics of living cultures. The archaeological record, however, is static; it can therefore be characterized in the following way:

(1) Any observable variation is a variation of *formal and/or spatial* attributes movement and development can only be inferred. This deficiency in the record apparently accounts for

the tendency, clearly recognizable in the typological paradigm, to explain most kinds of formal variation of artifacts as movement in time (typically as 'typological evolution'), and any spatial variation as movement in space (mostly as 'diffusion' of types or as migrations of peoples). The discipline's obsession with chronology, i.e. with the reconstruction of time coordinates, also seems to go back mainly to the lack of observable or recorded time.

(2) Archaeological artifacts and ecofacts are *non-functional*, i.e. their function cannot be observed. In this connection, function is to be understood as a dynamic relation between a fact and its surrounding physical environment. Thus, the function of an axe is cutting or chopping wood and other materials. Cutting and chopping are actions that necessarily take place in time, so they cannot be replaced either by repeated observation of the occurrence of axes with pieces of wood or by traces of work which can be spotted on the edges of the tools. The shape of an axe is a somewhat better guide but function again is different from shape; moreover, the dynamic (human) factor is missing here as well. Archaeologists usually do not hesitate to call their find an axe: they make the 'determination' either by means of analogy with some recent specimen or by comparison with another archaeological find whose function has been 'determined' previously. Both these procedures, despite their pragmatic success, present many difficulties. The analogy with modern things does not work if the difference in shape is too big. The stone axe, for example, is so much unlike the modern steel axe that the early finds of stone specimens were explained as thunder-bolts. The use of stipulatively determined function may lead to a cumulative error if it is applied several times in succession, and it may be extremely difficult to discover such a mistake. Many flint 'scrapers' probably belong to this category; the word 'scraper' expresses a presumed function and, in fact, for many archaeologists it is just a name for a set of formal attributes.

(3) Archaeological facts are *meaningless*. The meaning of an artifact is understood here as its relation to the social environment within which it operates. People do not use things merely to obtain their living (i.e. they do not merely exploit

the function of artifacts), they also use them as means of behaviour directed towards other people. As we have just noted, the function of axes is to cut; their meaning in the social sphere may be, for example, to express the division of labour (it is men in contrast to women who use axes), or to symbolize the division of men into warriors and possibly non-warriors (in the case of a battle-axe). These meanings disappear with the exit of facts from the living culture and, consequently, they cannot be observed. Thus, archaeological facts are meaningless in themselves: the relations between persons and groups of persons are entirely masked by relations between archaeological facts.

It should be stressed that meaning, as we use the term in this book, is an objective category reflecting objective relations, independent of the will of individuals. The natural division of labour (according to gender and age) is objectively connected with the use of certain tools which may but need not become symbols; the division of labour is the meaning of the tools. Symbols, which belong to the sphere of consciousness, are semiarbitrary and, as such, their significance can be stipulated within a community; they are not objective in the same way as meanings are.

(4) Archaeological facts are *silent* or *non-significant*. The significance of an artifact is conceived here as its relation to the realm of human consciousness or its role within the ideology of the particular epoch and place. While the meaning of axe may be in that it (objectively) separates social groups who use it from those who do not, the significance of the axe may be that it symbolizes a particular group of men (irrespective of whether they do use axes or not) just because the axe is connected with the group in the framework of the society's ideology.

Ideology depends heavily on natural languages and semiological systems in general. Even systems of semiarbitrary symbols and systems of artistic images (supposed to be non-arbitrary) are hardly comprehensible unless they have an interpretation in a natural language which correlates them with concepts of ideology.

I would not be as pessimistic as to exclude the possibility of guessing the significance of prehistoric artifacts but in any case the problem is very much like deciphering an unknown language with a little-known script. The example of Linear B Greek read by Ventris and Chadwick shows that this is not entirely impossible if the right kind of model is used (their model was a supposition that the language sought was a Greek dialect).

(5) Archaeological facts are *quantitatively unrepresentative*. I hope it has become sufficiently clear from section 3.4 of this chapter that most quantities observed by archaeologists in their record, if taken at face value, have little to do with quantitative relations within early communities; they simply reflect various measures of fragmentation, cumulation, reduction, etc. It may be only palaeontology that shares with archaeology this degree of quantitative deformation.

3.6 Inverse transformations

Most present-day archaeologists would like to grasp the life of ancient societies as fully as possible. No doubt, it will never be feasible to reproduce this life exactly; but, in any case, this is not the purpose of archaeology. The archaeological record, however, which is the only direct evidence of the human past in many instances, has been heavily transformed so that it consists of formal, non-functional, meaningless, silent and quantitatively unrepresentative things. Is it possible to resuscitate this record to make it 'tell history'?

It follows from the preceding paragraphs that there is no question of resuscitation: once dead, the archaeological record cannot be brought to life again. Too much has been lost through the exit transformation. At the same time it is undeniable that archaeological finds do contain much information about the past. Is there any possibility of reversing the effect of the transformations at least to the degree that the information on ancient life still contained in the finds would not disappear completely?

I believe I can answer the last question in the affirmative, and I share my belief with many colleagues. Those who find no way out of this dilemma are left to quite formal classificatory analysis with no aspirations to reconstruct any aspect of history on the basis of archaeological study. (The 'history' dealt with by pure diffusionists is in fact no human history at all: it is a history of dead things.)

I am going to use the term 'inverse transformations' while discussing procedures aimed at overcoming the adverse properties of the record brought about by the transformations. It might be more exact to employ the expression 'pseudo-inversion' as true inversion is impossible in view of the arguments of the preceding paragraphs. Despite this minor terminological inaccuracy I shall use the more simple expression 'inverse transformation' for a procedure which, in addition to the archaeological record, uses models derived from some theoretical discipline with observable dynamics.

My conviction that models coming from outside archaeology are needed in the task of reversing the transformations is based on the fact that archaeological finds are dead things, static systems, from which no dynamics can be recovered. No function, no meaning, no significance and no change can be derived from the finds themselves. If this seems to be possible, it is only because archaeologists often use a kind of consensus when approaching their finds, and this is usually some kind of a simple unsophisticated model.

Inverse transformation in the sense used here is, of course, more or less identical with the archaeological method, whose task it is to find ways of explaining change, function, meaning and significance in the archaeological record. Because of the specific properties of the archaeological record, so much unlike the properties of the records studied by history or various branches of cultural anthropology, our discipline is characterized by a number of methodological peculiarities.

The use of models is a deductive procedure within the course of archaeological reasoning. But are there any steps in inverse transformation which are more or less inductive, i.e. such that they do not necessitate models? If so, the inverse transformations could start with a sort of criticism of records 'uninfluenced' by knowledge derived from outside. However, we do not find any such inductive element to start with. Thus, it is up to analysis to become the first step of the archaeological method.

4

Archaeological analysis

The archaeological method presents two basic problems: (1) how to get from the archaeological record, i.e. from the contemporary material things belonging to the *material world* around us, to the *concepts of mind* which are the building stones of our theories; (2) how to make statements on the *live* ancient society overcoming the *deadness* of the archaeological record. While the second problem is solved by interpretation, the first one is answered by archaeological analysis and synthesis. The transition from things to concepts cannot be realized without a chain of notions such as entities/qualities, points/traits and items/variables. The use of models plays a central role in the process of answering both questions, thus indicating the importance of deduction throughout the archaeologial method. The present chapter discusses archaeological analysis.

Many scientists are inclined to describe almost anything they do as analysis. This attitude, no doubt, represents a survival of the positivist approach to the scientific work, as the first and foremost goal of a 'positive' science was a detailed anatomy of scientific facts. Analysis, however, means 'decomposition' and this chapter will use the word exclusively in this sense.

Archaeological analysis is basically of two kinds. First of all, it is the process of the material decomposition of sites during excavations in the field (cf. section 4.3). Second, it is the mental decomposition of finds which have already been placed outside their original context. The two varieties are similar in many respects, but the first kind of analysis is in a sense primary.

Analysis has always been the realm of empricism and induction. It has been pretended that description of the archaeological record is achieved by an objective mapping of 'finds' into a set of properties which are selected independently of previous archaeological theories. Then, archaeological concepts are obtained inductively by generalizing on the basis of the description.

I shall argue that despite the fact that analysis very often looks like this, the real process of obtaining archaeologial knowledge is very different. The archaeological context is analysed first into the entities and qualities, then into points and traits; it is only at the end of the analytical endeavour that the 'objective' spatial and formal categories emerge.

4.1   The archaeological context

The whole to be decomposed during analysis will be referred to as the *archaeological context*. This is to be understood as a set of archaeological records which have been selected to become the object of analysis. The *identification* of the context is therefore the first task of the archaeological method. In practice it often seems that it can be performed quite easily: it is sufficient to go to a site (on the condition that the position of the site is known), to dig there for some time, and a context comes automatically to light. Another common procedure, which is even more simple, consists of studying finds in museums; visiting libraries or archaeological archives instead of going to sites or collections is still another common way of obtaining the required contexts.

From the point of view of theory, however, all this is not a straightforward procedure: the question arises on what basis it can be recognized that the set of things before the archaeologist can be considered as an archaeological context? Clearly, this must become one of the elementary *assumptions* of the whole method; it is sometimes made on the basis of previous knowledge of similar 'contexts' (positive selection), sometimes on the basis of a suspicion that the things lying before the archaeologist are man-made and not modern (negative selection). The identification of a context is not yet archaeologial analysis: it is in fact the world around us which we analyse in this phase of our endeavour to find an archaeologial context.

Once one assumes that a set of objects is an archaeological context, it is time to perform analysis, synthesis and interpretation to confirm or to reject the assumption. This may take a few seconds, if there is a close analogy (or model) with which the 'context' can be compared; in some instances, however, even detailed discussion does not help. There are many examples of whole collections of 'stones' which may, but need not, be prehistoric stone industries and, consequently, need not constitute a context.

The identification of a context is used with sets of records which form a still undivided whole; finds from excavations are a typical example. There is another way of creating contexts: it is the *specification of contexts* which consists of assembling individual parts of the record which is already there, according to a selected criterion. This procedure requires some kind of previous analysis (some kind of identification must have preceded as well) and it is typical of contexts created on the basis of museum finds.

The set of archaeological records that aspires to become a context must consist of more than one element. A single, unique object, which archaeologists are unable to insert into a specifiable context, cannot be analysed and, consequently, it cannot be explained (not even dated). In some instances it *seems* that archaeologists do analyse individual things (such as a magnificent torque found during sand digging) but in reality they always try to create (to specify) a context of 'analogical' personal ornaments and other similar objects. On finding a unique object, archaeologists try to place it into one (or several) of the contexts they have ready in stock; it is these contexts that are subsequently analysed, not the isolated object.

There is an important question of whether archaeologists are entitled to specify their contexts according to their free will. Although the answer may seem to be to the affirmative, it clearly leads nowhere to enjoy this freedom excessively. The more coherent is the context from the point of view of its original purpose, the greater is the probability that the whole work will be successful. Here again, the cohesion of a context must be assumed before the analysis starts; it is only later that it can be iteratively improved.

The size of an archaeological context is a parameter which should not be underestimated. If the quantity of its elements is small, it often has the advantage of being homogeneous; at the same time, however, the structures derived from such a context tend to be unreliable (statistically insignificant). It may not always help to specify a big context; if it is heterogeneous (e.g. complexes collected from a number of sites over a large territory), its structures would be hidden in the 'noise' produced by the heterogeneity. These facts present quite a problem with cemeteries in most parts of prehistoric Europe: they were small (because the prehistoric communities were small) and by combining several of them one frequently gets heterogeneous conglomerates.

I am using a two-way system of analytical units (cf. Table 4.1). The basic horizontal dichotomy is between entities and qualities (which are often called attributes). *Entities* are conceived as separate and distinct objects of the archaeological record while *qualities* are properties of such objects. The former refer to the spatial aspect of the units, the latter to their formal aspect. There are problems as to how to treat fragments and/or parts of complex artifacts (for example, a plough share). Also, in some cases at least, there is the problem of distinguishing between an entity and a quality. There is no sharp division between the two: the blade of an axe and its handle can be conceived either as two parts of an (arti)fact, i.e. two separate entities, or as two attributes of a single entity. Such problems are not easy to overcome theoretically, but they may not present serious difficulties in concrete research applications.

4.2   Units of analysis

The basic units of analysis to be described in the following paragraphs are differentiated according to the level of abstraction from their function, meaning and significance and, at the same time, according to their concreteness. It may appear that the units at the three levels to be described are more or less identical and no dividing line need be drawn between them. This was more or less the position of traditional archaeology, leading to chaos in the question of observ-

Table 4.1. *A system of analytical units.*

	entities	qualities
structuring elements	structuring entities	structuring qualities
subjects of structures	points	traits
data	items	variables

ability and the role of deduction in the very first stage of the archaeological method. Without clearly distinguishing between the structuring elements, subjects of structures and items of data, it appears to me to be impossible to understand properly how the units of archaeological analysis can be at the same time empirically observed objects and structures, derived from models.

There are three horizontal divisions in Table 4.1. The first of them is headed 'structuring elements', classed into 'structuring entities' and 'structuring qualities'. The ability to structure contexts derives from the fact that these elements are not formal but, by comparison with models, are endowed with function, meaning and/or significance. The second line is headed 'subjects of structures'. What is meant is that individual items and variables (i.e. the entities and qualities of the record) are assigned to structural elements; as a result the individual facts are *subjected* to structures and thus become their particular instances. By means of their comparison with models, the subjects of structures are interpreted as to their function, meaning and/or significance. The resulting concepts, described as points and traits, seem to be rather important. The third line (headed 'data') contains the observational units which abstract from any purpose; they are the formal units of analysis, believed by the empiricists to be the 'objective' starting point of scientific analysis.

As to the terminology of the following paragraphs, it originated in several steps in my previous attempts to untangle these important questions. I have tried to accommodate the terms to those already existing in the field. In some cases such as entity, attribute, data, variable and (possibly) item, my usage does not seem to differ substantially from the widely accepted meaning of the words. I have attempted to choose, for the 'observable' units of analysis, terms that archaeology shares with other empirically orientated disciplines (data, item, variable). As to the 'subjects of structures', a newly introduced category, I am using terms which either have not yet been used in archaeology (points, bodies, figures) or have been rarely applied in recent years (trait).

'Structuring elements' are in fact manifestations of structures, one of the central concepts of this volume, which will be analysed in the next chapter in more detail. I do not insist on any of the terms of Table 4.1, but I believe that the concepts standing behind them may be of interest. Practical archaeologists will probably not use more than a few of them.

4.2.1   *Structuring elements*

Once archaeologists have identified or specified their context, they formulate more or less explicitly its *original model* (i.e. the model which stands at the origin of the method; it is sometimes described as the preliminary model). This can be fairly abstract, i.e. poor in properties, which is natural considering the fact that it has to be formulated before the first phase of analysis. The model may be expressed, for example, by the following statement: 'The context we are going to analyse is a usual Corded Ware cemetery of Central Europe.' This says a lot to those who are acquainted with the culture group; first of all it suggests the selection of archaeological entities and qualities to begin with. We may now know what to mark out on the skeletons, which classes of pottery can be expected in the graves, etc. However, if the cemetery to be analysed were the first of its kind and nothing were known about it in advance, it would be necessary to formulate the model in much more general terms.

Structuring entities and qualities are such elements of the

context that are able to order it or, in other words, to generate its structures. They are formed by abstract classes of the record and its properties; examples are amphorae, weapons, houses, components, corded decoration, distance between two villages, etc. It is a quite 'natural' and logical demand that the context be decomposed in terms of just such elements. Archaeologists are not interested in *any kind* of finds and their properties, as it is only the structuring elements that are passed to structures and thus explained in the phase of interpretation. Without the original model, which to some degree presumes the results of the application of the archaeological method to the context, it would be impossible to decide, for example, which properties of the finds might be important for the synthesis of archaeological structures in the next step of the method.

From what has been told up to now it may be clear that the logical status of the two kinds of structuring elements, i.e. of the structuring entities and qualities, is in fact quite near to that of a kind of elementary archaeological structure; their most simple forms apparently match linguistic phonemes. When archaeologists approach their contexts for the first time, they assume these elements to be possible elementary structures; it is up to further steps of the method and its further iterations to make this assumption more probable. Let us note that such a conception of the role of the original models at the beginning of the archaeological method leaves enough space for the concreteness of contexts: it does not impose the structuring entities and qualities on the context as definitive structures known in advance (what in fact traditional archaeology mostly does). These entities and qualities are only *suggested as possible* structuring elements.

When empiricists distinguish anything like our structuring entities and qualities, they conceive of them as sets of things or sets of the properties of things. The individual instances of the two concepts then become materially concrete objects; the 'grave', in an empiricist vision, is simply a common denomination for a great number of particular features excavated in the field. In the conception accepted in this book, the structuring elements are not mere names for sets of things; they are objects at the level of structures, i.e. abstract notions expressing the socially important pattern contained in the finds. As already noted, structures cannot be separated from the things through which they exist; it is for this reason that the structuring entities and those things that are their concrete manifestations are sometimes identified. This should not hide the principal difference between the structuring elements and the 'things' of the archaeological record.

As already noted, the structuring elements of a context are of two types. The *structuring entities* are patterns of individual 'things', i.e. patterns of relatively independent real objects, which are as a rule discontinuous and spatially delimited; it is assumed that they carried out some function, had some meaning and/or significance. The decomposition of a context into structuring entities is sometimes very simple (e.g. in the case of most cemeteries) but in many instances it may be a quite complicated task which can only be accomplished on the basis of arbitrary decisions. The number of structuring entities in a context may be very great but it is finite. Within traditional archaeology, it was usually the task of spatial analysis to distinguish entities, but spatial analysis is not entirely identical with the analysis of entities as discussed below.

The *structuring qualities* are the properties of structuring entities. Every entity, even the most simple one, has an infinite number of properties; archaeologists select those which they believe to have the structuring ability. It is assumed that the structuring qualities reflect some function, meaning and/or significance. Within traditional methodology it was the role of formal analysis to find the qualities of a context.

4.2.2   Archaeological points and traits

What archaeologists observe in their record are not abstract notions but quite concrete material objects. The structuring entities and qualities are structures; in the course of their analysis we need designations for the *individual instances of particular structuring entities and qualities* or for the subjects of structures (for example for individual pots which 'contain' the structuring entity 'amphora'). I shall therefore introduce some new concepts which should make it easier to operate further discussion of the theme. The concepts, being derived from mathematics, are able to formalize to some degree the analysis of the structuring elements. In the case of entities, which will be discussed first, the complementary notions are archaeologial point and archaeological body.

The *(archaeological) point* is a concrete instance of a structuring entity consisting of a set of geometrical points (elements of three-dimensional Euclidean space). The point is a discrete and spatially delimited part of the archaeological record. It follows that the point has finite dimensions. Examples of archaeological points are individual artifacts, ecofacts and/or their fragments, storage pits, graves, individual dwelling sites, etc. A set of archaeological points such that it is itself a point will be called the *archaeological body*. A body which consists of a single point will be referred to as the *elementary point*. An example of the archaeological body is a dwelling site consisting of storage pits and houses (which are again bodies of lower rank); the pits themselves contain fragments of pottery each of which is an elementary point.

In the course of space analysis in archaeology one often uses Cartesian coordinates to define points in Euclidean space. Such points, of course, cannot be identified with the archaeological points as described above. Similarly, when an archaeological feature or some other object is divided into arbitrary parts (plots, etc.), the parts cannot be considered to constitute archaeological points.

Concepts such as point and body may seem unusual in archaeology but they offer some measure of compatibility with certain parts of mathematics. The mathematical point is an object in a multidimensional space, which is also the case with archaeological points. Each mathematical point has a number of coordinates which determine its position in relation to other points; we shall see later that archaeological points also have their coordinates fulfilling more or less the same function. It will be explained in the following paragraphs that there are also agreements between set-theoretical and archaeological relations obtained on the basis of the concept of archaeological points and bodies. These space relations enable more exact definitions of certain well-known archaeologial concepts.

From the formal point of view, the analysis of structuring qualities is quite analogous to that of structuring entities. A *trait* is a particular instance of a structuring quality characterizing an archaeologial point. The *figure* is a set of traits such that it is itself a trait. The *elementary trait* is a figure which consists of a single element.

The technical elements of decoration on pottery, such as incised lines or cord impressions, are examples of elementary traits. Other examples of traits are as follows: the shapes of the necks of beakers (cylindrical, conical, funnel-shaped, bulging, etc.), the length and width of a house, the number of vessels in a grave, etc. The amount of radiocarbon in a piece of charcoal is also a trait. Examples of figures are: decoration motifs (consisting of a set of decorative elements), pottery shapes (integrating traits such as the shapes of neck, shoulders, belly, lower part and bottom), the area of a cemetery (a sum of the areas of individual grave groups), the number of flints in a site (consisting of the numbers of flints in individual features of the site).

4.2.3   *Archaeological data*

Both structuring entities and points could not fulfil their function within the framework of the discipline's methodology if they did not contain the element of interpretation, and the same is true of the pair structuring qualities-traits. The interpretive aspect, however, is not needed in some of the 'inductive' stages of the method such as description or generation of structures. To describe a sword effectively it is, of course, necessary to consider its function and possible (or probable) meaning and significance, but once these problems have been settled and a list of traits established, both the sword and its traits can be stripped of their interpretive aspects and defined quite formally. The words 'sword', 'blade', 'point', etc. will usually be retained but turned into more or less geometrical concepts. Prehistoric 'bowls' or 'jugs' are examples of such formalized categories where the original function of the vessels plays no role.

I shall distinguish by means of the term 'item' between the points of the record (which do contain some measure of interpretation) and the pieces of data in the sense discussed in the following paragraphs. The archaeological record can be seen both in the light of structuring entities/points and as simple 'items' devoid of any interpretation. However, by separating the archaeological record from its function, meaning and significance one creates a special archaeological language (Gardin 1979) which is formal but well suited to express observation. Points are turned into observable *items* and traits into observable *variables*; the relations between individual items and between individual variables can also be formalized.

When looking for a set of observable characteristics of the archaeologial record, it will be necessary to specify what should be understood under the term 'observability'. Observable items and variables of the archaeological record are those which, to be identified, do not require a reference to archaeological categories endowed with function, meaning significance and/or change, i.e. the categories presupposing the time coordinate. Concepts derived from geometry, physics, chemistry and various branches of natural science are allowed free access, but concepts that make use of 'historical time' are forbidden when analysing the context on this level.

Thus, for example, 'inhumation grave' represents a valid concept (a possible denotation for an archaeological item) because it can be identified on the basis of observation plus a few formal definitions containing exclusively non-archaeological terms, for example as 'a pit containing human bones in anatomical order'. By contrast, a 'rich grave' or an 'altar' is less satisfactory because neither 'richness' nor the rites proving the function of the 'altar' can be observed. Both 'rich graves' and 'altars', however, are valid archaeological points. Once we set up by definition that rich graves, for example, are those that contain at least five artifacts, we have created a formal criterion on the basis of which 'rich graves' become archaeological items. It is, of course, obvious that this kind of richness has little to do with what would be described by that term in the course of archaeological explanations.

We have followed the way from structuring entities/ qualities as derived from models through points/traits to items/variables, which empiricists declare to be the basis of archaeologial analysis. According to the argument presented in the foregoing paragraphs, they are derivatives whose names denote formal concepts by no means identical with the concepts connected with those words in any living culture.

Where the difference has some sense, the following concepts should be distinguished:

(1) the archaeological things/properties (things of the outer world and their properties as perceived by our senses);

(2) the structuring entities/qualities (the order or pattern contained in the archaeological things and properties, obtained from the original model);

(3) the archaeological points/traits as particular concrete instances of the structuring entities/qualities;

(4) the items/variables representing formalized points/traits which are observable in the sense defined above.

On the one hand, it is clear that the items and variables are not the starting points of analysis but rather its results; they are derived by way of deduction. If this is not fully realized, there is a danger that the deduction (which is unavoidable anyway) will be performed half-consciously and, as a result, will get beyond the control of the scientific method. On the other hand, it cannot be denied that data (i.e. the items and variables) are valid concepts and cannot be fully replaced either by the structuring elements (i.e. the structuring entities and qualities) or by the subjects of structures (i.e. the points and traits).

Archaeological items are spatial units of the archaeologial record (facts taken from their formal point of view) while the variables represent its formal aspects. As a result, analysis and synthesis based on items is more or less identical with what is usually described as spatial analysis, and the work done with variables is often equivalent with the so called formal analysis. The analytical methods which end by establishing items are termed, in this volume, the analysis of entities and those ending in variables are referred to as the analysis of qualities.

It was clearly realized at the beginning of the New Archaeology that it is only spatial and formal properties that can be observed in the archaeological record (Spaulding 1960). There are no other kinds of properties to be observed archaeologically. It is interesting to note how many archaeologists still maintain, in defiance of logical facts, that time also can be observed, e.g. by means of stratigraphy or through the radio-carbon dating method. If it were so, the whole archaeological method would be very different (more easy in many respects).

Unfortunately, it is clear that stratigraphy is simply a spatial relationship *interpreted* in terms of time, and radiocarbon dating is just inferred from measurements of formal prop-erties of organic materials (their isotopic composition). Time is only reflected either in the spatial distribution of the record or in its form (e.g. in the case of typological evolution). Let us note that other dimensions of the archaeological record, for example the social dimension, are also unobservable.

The notion of formal properties (or, better, of variables) is very wide. It covers physical dimensions of artifacts and ecofacts (length, width, thickness, weight), shape (very many possibilities depending on the class of the artifact or the ecofact), material (including its chemical composition), colour, and the 'aesthetic' treatment of the artifact, most aspects of which are described as 'decoration'. The enumer-ated groups of variables are only examples, though the most important ones, used here for the purpose of general description.

Strictly speaking, the observation of formal variables is a matter for disciplines other than archaeology. Taking measurements and weighing, as well as the study of hardness and even of colours, is the proper task for physics, the study of shapes for geometry. The study of materials should be (and often is) done by mineralogy, petrography, chemistry, nuclear chemistry, etc. Even the decoration of pots belongs rather to the competence of some branch of semiology. I am unable to find a single group of variables which would be specifically archaeological.

Quite often, however, the height of vessels is measured by archaeologists themselves because this is a fairly simple task for which a physicist is unnecessary. The description of arti-facts is somewhat more complicated in other instances, but it is still viable for an archaeologist to learn how to do it prop-erly. There is a tendency, however, to leave the study of most of the ecofacts to competent specialists; in some cases, such as thermoluminescence, it is not desirable to all to try to replace the scientist or the technician. The main reason why archaeologists try to substitute for specialists is the lack of funds; were it not for this fact, they would probably leave a lot of the descriptive work to others.

What, then, is the role of the archaeologist in the analysis of his or her finds, if their competent description (wherever more complicated) should be done by non-archaeologists? The answer has already been given: it is the selection of the structuring entities and qualities and their integration into the framework of archaeological method and theory.

The situation is similar in the case of spatial analysis. It is often believed that 'careful' spatial analysis should be based on Cartesian coordinates for almost any find. Such coordinates are, of course, welcome media for many accurate studies but the substance of the analysis of entities rests with the specification of the archaeological data and their relations and functions. By the way, this was how many traditional archaeologists understood spatial analysis: to determine the context in which an artifact had been found and to examine with which other artifacts it had come to light. Traditional archaeology, of course, also produced many maps where individual finds were sometimes stripped of their space relationships.

The attractiveness of the Cartesian coordinates (and the maps resulting from them) for many modern archaeologists may be supported by their 'objective' appearance; they seem to be almost entirely free of the assumptions which so heavily influence what has been described as the analysis of structuring entities in the preceding paragraphs. Especially when followed by mathematical 'analysis' of the 'objective' numbers, the coordinates seem to represent one of the safest points in archaeology. The finds whose coordinates lie at the basis of such studies, however, cannot escape being hidden archaeological points (with entities behind); moreover, they rarely cluster in such a way that no arbitrary decisions are necessary during their delimitation.

One reason why so many archaeologists believe that it is the items and variables which they begin with, is the indisputable truth that they often manipulate a set of 'all imaginable' properties in the search for new variables. Despite the fact that the number of these properties is theoretically infinite, it is often not possible to find, on the basis of the currently used archaeological 'technology', more than a few distances between various parts of a vessel such that they could be measured repeatedly on a larger sample of pottery. In this situation, archaeologists experiment by adding new variables to those already in use; the selection may be done according to the criterion 'what else is objectively observable and repeatedly recordable' rather than by deduction from a theoretical model.

Such a procedure of searching for additional variables is possible because the items and variables, once they are abstracted from points and traits, become relatively autonomous; they look like observed empirical reality, which is independent of previous knowledge. No objections can be raised against this 'non-theoretical' search unless one believes that this is the general research strategy adopted for the acquisition of the 'empirical' elements. New variables that later prove to lead to important new qualities may be suggested in a dream or hallucination but most of them are certainly not.

This is the place to mention the assumption of many archaeologists that the best approach to the problem of variable selection is to include *'all of them'* and then to run a sample of data, described by means of this complete set of variables, through a computer program (factor analysis or another method from the same family) to see what to retain for further desciption. This procedure appears very 'objective' and it seemingly removes the necessity of using non-empirical knowledge. However, it is impossible in practice because the number of properties of any natural object (and archaeological facts are objects of nature) is infinite; thus, the list of 'all possible variables' can never be complete. Also, what is described in such a case are the usual traditional variables which already proved to be structuring elements of many similar contexts analysed previously. Thus, the method of starting with a 'complete' set of variables is unfeasible and, in practice, it does not lead to greater objectivity (if this is conceived as independence on preceding theories).

Moreover, the illusion of the possibility of using the complete set of variables mostly rests on the naïve assumption that what traditional archaeology recorded through observation by the naked eye or with the help of very simple aids (such as a measuring tape or callipers) is the only choice. Modern computer-aided and/or automated methods of recording natural properties of things make it easy to characterize any material object by means of a large number of properties, and the development and accessibility to archaeologists of such equipment will no doubt greatly increase in the future.

Using a system of digitized image recording of artifacts by means of a computer (cf. Plog and Carlson 1989) it is possible to obtain a theoretically unlimited number of measurements of any number of archaeological data in a second, and there is no reason in principle why this number of measurements could not be doubled or multiplied by a factor of ten in the near future. Equipment for making exact chemical analyses of pottery sherds automatically (and for feeding the results directly into a computer) may not yet exist but, here again, there is no reason in principle why it could not be constructed if there were no economic considerations. The huge memories and very fast processors of modern computers create the material basis for an effective management of so much data.

I have used the example of the shape and chemical composition of artifacts more or less because they are variables generally accepted by present-day archaeology. Material objects, however, have many more natural properties which are already known at present but cannot be exploited in full because of the forbidding cost of the equipment and the procedures necessary to record the results. An even greater number of natural properties of archaeological data have probably not yet been discovered.

There is an important question whether so much information is really needed in archaeology. The well-known experience is that many archaeological variables are strongly correlated; this means that, in many respects, almost any variable can be replaced by another one or by a group of variables without any great loss of information. Thus, for example, many male La Tène graves in Central Europe contain both an iron sword and remains of a shield. At the same time there are some sword graves without a shield and shield graves with a spear but no sword. Unless derived from one another or unless one is an integral and obligatory part of the other, two items or two variables cannot be 100 per cent correlated. It may be difficult, however, to prove that there is a non-random difference, if the context is small. Thus, the extent of the context selected depends on the number of variables. Leaving the context unchanged, in analysing it into even more elements is not helpful.

4.2.4 Relations between entities and qualities

The mathematical concept of (binary) relation is quite simple. Let us assume two sets, for example a set of all battle-axes A and a set of all beakers B of a particular context. Now let us form the so-called Cartesian product A × B of the two sets, i.e. let us form all ordered pairs such that one of its elements is a battle-axe and the other is a beaker. We obtain pairs such as (battle-axe 1, beaker 1), (battle-axe 3, beaker 15), etc. A mathematical relation is any subset of the set of all the possible pairs. From the non-formal point of view the subset is selected to fulfil some specified condition (for example, it may contain all pairs consisting of a battle-axe and a beaker such that the two artifacts have been found in one grave). As a result, (binary) relations are sets of ordered pairs, which is another – and possibly more exact – meaning of the common notion.

Any possible combination of any number of ordered pairs selected from the total set of all ordered pairs (the Cartesian product) defines a relation. Thus, the theoretical number of relations is tremendous even for quite small original sets; only a small proportion of them can be meaningful. The subset of ordered pairs believed to be significant for the solution of a specific problem is therefore selected on the basis of a well-defined criterion, for example 'relation A between beakers and amphorae holds for all pairs of vessels composed of a beaker and an amphora such that the pair has been found in the same grave'. In other words it can be put as follows: there is a relation (of incidence) between beakers and amphorae found in the same grave. Some of the most common relations between archaeological entities will be discussed in the following paragraphs.

Insertion is the relation between an entity and a set of entities in which it is contained, for example between a body and a point. The point is an element of the body, and the body contains the point (it is a set of points). Spatial analysis in archaeology often begins by defining the insertions which order individual entities (e.g. points and bodies) into hierarchies. The archaeological context of a cemetery (the highest-ranking body in this particular case) can be decomposed into grave groups (lower-order bodies), groups into graves, graves into grave goods, grave pits and (possibly) the skeletons; the grave goods consist of individual artifacts which are elementary points. All the links of the chain enumerated in the example are joined by the relation of insertion. From the mathematical point of view this relation is partial ordering, which in fact makes it possible to transfer to the insertion some interesting properties of an important class of mathematical objects.

The relation between two entities of the same set of entities is called *incidence*. This is sometimes described as common occurrence and it has been of great importance to archaeology, especially since the end of the nineteenth century. Examples of this relation include the coincidence of two or more types in an archaeological complex, the relation between the elements of a context, etc. From the mathematical point of view it is so-called equivalence.

Exclusion is a relation between two entities which belong to different sets of entities. If the sets of entities are, for example two different archaeological components, and the two selected entities are two sets of sherds belonging to different pottery types, the fact of their exclusion is certainly significant.

Still another spatial relation, exploited in archaeology for many decades, is *substitution*. It is the relation between two archaeological entities that occupy (at least partially) the same place in Euclidean space. It cannot happen otherwise than that one of the entities substitutes for the other; a special case of this relation is clearly the example of classical stratigraphy.

From the mathematical point of view substitution is partial ordering which, in this particular case, can often be used for chronological ordering.

Mathematical function is another concept which helps archaeological analysis become better defined. A mathematical function is a Cartesian product of a set by itself where each pair of the product is assigned a real number. Thus, while relations are sets of ordered pairs, mathematical functions are sets of ordered triples; apparently both are similar objects. Considering archaeological entities such as sites of a region, it is possible to join each pair of sites with a real number measuring their distance. The distance is an example of a (mathematical) function in archaeology; all the distances between sites of a region can be easily arranged into a matrix.

The example of the preceding paragraph described a function where the numbers (the distances) could be measured directly. There are many cases where the numbers of a function have to be calculated. Correlation matrices and many other objects of that kind are in fact functions from the mathematical point of view.

Similarly, as in the case of entities, a number of *relations* can be defined with archaeological qualities. Insertion is the relation between qualities and sets of qualities (e.g. between traits and figures); here again there results a hierarchy of qualities (decorative element, motif, pattern, decoration system). Incidence is the relation between elements of the same set of qualities, e.g. between particular decorative elements of the same motif. Exclusion is the relation between qualities coming from different sets of qualities, e.g. between decorative motifs and the surface colour of pots. Even substitution can be defined, being exemplified, for example, by the re-use of artifacts.

In addition to distances which are frequently used to characterize qualities, other kinds of functions are also well known. Among those widely deployed let us name at least the number of 'common occurrences' (the number of overall incidences) of various kinds of qualities. Measurements taken on vessels can be imagined as 'results' of functions: the height of a pot is in fact the distance between the bottom and the rim.

4.2.5   Classes of entities and qualities

Items are the elementary units of the archaeological record (i.e. facts) considered in their formalized aspect; as such, their most general categories are artifacts, ecofacts and natural facts. The division of artifacts into classes based on their assumed function (tools, weapons, pottery, etc.) has already been mentioned; this division is often simply transferred to items, forgetting about the function and meaning of the terms and taking them as designations for observational categories. But not all the units of the record can be considered to constitute data. Complexes, components and settlement areas, for example, cannot be recognized on the basis of observation alone and, as a result, they rather belong among structuring entities and/or points.

Individual items, such as the beaker from grave 12 at Vikletice, could be described by means of a symbol of a purely formal language (e.g. 'VB12') but this is not the procedure preferred by archaeologists; they tend to exploit the natural language describing their items by means of the same words as those used for the points/bodies assumed to correspond to the items. This practice is responsible for the common error of the general public that what is described as a 'stone blade' in a museum show case was really used in the neolithic in more or less the same way as blades in our contemporary life: many archaeologists even believe this.

Some of the archaeological denotations for data are semiformal. The already quoted 'Vikletice grave 12' belongs to this class: 'grave' is derived from the interpretation of the corresponding archaeological point, but 'Vikletice' and '12' are formal designations; the non-formal equivalent would be 'grave of Mr Xxx interred in the cemetery of village Yyy' (where 'Xxx' and 'Yyy' stand for words of the prehistoric language spoken in northwest Bohemia in the eneolithic period).

There are instances when archaeologists are so uncertain about the original function of what they find during excavations that they have to describe their findings in a completely formal way. An example is 'feature 102' which says nearly nothing about the interpretation of the respective piece of data. There is a tendency, however, to replace such expressions by more 'human' words at least when preparing a report for publication.

Summing up, the basic classification of archaeological items is according to their assumed (or stipulated) function. This would not be harmful if every archaeologist were aware of this fact and used this classification in the proper way, realizing that points and items are two very different concepts even if they are sometimes denoted by the same words.

Variables selected by archaeologists are classified according to a number of criteria. One of the most common divisions is that taking into account the material, shape, linear dimensions, weight, surface treatment, presence of symbols or signs, etc. This seems to be the most 'natural' classification and, indeed, historically it was the earliest one applied. It was not purely qualitative as it also partly consisted of numbers, but its quantitative aspect was of limited value: archaeologists could rarely be seen manipulating the numbers other than the calculation of percentages.

With the advent of mathematical methods another classification became widespread: variables and qualities in general could now be classed either as *nominal* (formerly called qualitative) or *cardinal* (formerly called quantitative). Individual entities were 'measured' on either the nominal or cardinal *scales*. The nominal scale, a typical example of which is colour, could not be meaningfully expressed in numbers but it produced a set of *states or values* (blue, red, purple, etc.) which could not be ordered (compared according to their magnitude). In some instances, however, the now-admired cardinal scale could be 'approximated' by creating an *ordinal scale* in which it was at least possible to order the individual states according to their magnitude (beakers were small, medium or large).

All *cardinal qualities* are not of the same nature and value. Weight, for example, is given by numbers, by means of which it can be uniquely and objectively determined which of two artifacts is heavier. Also, zero means 'nothing' and in this sense it is objective. Coordinates, however, have no objective zero (its position is chosen arbitrarily). Similarly, it is only within the given system of coordinates that it can be determined which coordinate is greater and which is smaller, as this depends on where the origin of the system is placed and in which direction it is measured. Especially dangerous are numbers such as degrees which have a limited set of values: 360° is followed by 0° so that an average of measurements that cluster around this point has no real sense.

Another scale which is of great importance in archaeology is the *dichotomic* or *binary* scale. It measures qualities which have only two states, usually presence and absence. These two states may be represented by numbers 1 and 0 and thus turned into 'real' numbers subject to normal arithmetic operations. The dichotomic qualities are sometimes, without any proper reason, classed among the nominal qualities and this makes them seemingly unsuitable as data for more sophisticated mathematical methods. However, as will be shown in examples given in the next chapter, dichotomic attributes do well in most instances.

It is, of course, the *nominal attributes* that are considered to be most characteristic of the archaeological record. These qualities have more than two states: within the variable 'shape of neck (of a vessel)' it may be possible to distinguish values such as 'conical', 'cylindrical', or 'funnel-shaped'. As a rule, only one of these values occurs on each vessel so that they are mutually exclusive: if a beaker has a cylindrical neck, it cannot have a conical neck at the same time.

It is for this reason that nominal qualities cannot be turned into dichotomic by simply taking each of their states as a new dichotomic quality (e.g. by eliminating the 'shape of the neck' and replacing it with 'conical neck', 'cylindrical neck' and 'funnel-shaped neck'). If we tried to calculate a correlation between 'conical necks' and 'cylindrical necks', we would obtain zero for their common occurrence (as the two attributes never occur together) and, in consequence of this, a highly significant negative correlation. This being the consequence of the logical incompatibility of the two neck shapes, the zero is in fact no real number and the correlation has no proper sense. This is a principal difference from the case of two dichotomic attributes such as 'the presence of a beaker (in a grave)' and 'the presence of an amphora (in a grave)'. There is no logical reason why a beaker could not turn up in the same grave as an amphora; in consequence of this, their zero common occurrence really means 'no occurrence'. The described property of the nominal qualities causes (mathematical) non-linearity and non-metricity resulting in the exclusion of most of the effective methods of archaeological synthesis.

The cardinal scale can easily be transformed into the ordinal, and this one again into the nominal scale. For example, the 'volume of amphorae' can be expressed in litres (cardinal scale) or in the ordered sequence large, medium, small (ordinal sale), and by forgetting about this order one obtains a nominal scale (small amphora, medium-sized amphora, large amphora). Transforming the scales in this way, one necessarily loses information. Because of this loss it is unlikely that the opposite progression, i.e. from the nominal scale to the cardinal, would ever be possible. It can be imagined, however, that nominal attributes could be replaced by one or several cardinal attributes each; in this case, of course, the information would increase.

The attribute 'neck shape (of a vessel)' can also be described, in addition to the three nominal states, by an index expressing the shape, by a series of numbers measuring the diameter at several equidistant points, or by a mathematical equation representing the shape as a curve. Decomposing the attribute into the nominal states is certainly the most simple one of these procedures and, considering the traditional ways of measuring and recording, the quickest. At the same time, it throws away much possibly important information included in the degree in which the neck is conical or funnel-shaped. It is already feasible, and this feasibility may grow rapidly in the near future, to take detailed measurements (and to perform the necessary computations) as fast as to accomplish the traditional (and often somewhat subjective) classification of the neck shape into the three nominal states. In this respect, at least, the way to replacing nominal qualities by means of cardinal ones is open. There emerge some new problems, not solved by the currently used mathematical methods, if basically one quality is expressed by means of a whole set of numbers.

As far as I know, the question whether all nominal qualities can be expressed as cardinal qualities, has not yet been solved. In most instances it is certainly impossible to describe one nominal variable by a single number; at the same time it appears to be feasible to approximate any imaginable quality by a series of real numbers or by a mathematical equation.

4.2.6   Units of analysis and reality

There is an interesting problem of how the units, obtained in the course of the archaeological analysis, relate to the units as recognized by ancient peoples. Do the two sets of units coincide, and should they coincide at all for a 'true' picture of the past to be achieved? This is more or less a question of theory. Much emphasis has recently been placed on the cognitive aspect of past creativeness and on the role of individuals in forming their world (Hodder 1986). If this approach is followed logically, the concepts created in the minds of past producers would be decisive, and the best analytical units would certainly be the units recognized by the producers and users of the ancient artifacts themselves.

Where it is possible to compare the concepts derived by means of the usual archaeological methods from the archaeo-logical record with the concepts expressed in the words used by producers of the 'record', one frequently finds a consider-able discrepancy. This discrepancy is not absolute but it seems to point to the fact that the makers and users of artifacts do not feel it necessary to analyse their behaviour rationally.

It is obvious that many spheres of human behaviour, though important for an archaeologist, cannot find any reflection in the minds of the subjects of the behaviour. Many important *choices* are predetermined by a set of possibilities given by the historical or natural conditions. A neolithic farmer could not have bought steel to make a better axe, and could only have used the clay found within his reach to produce pottery. He could not influence the chemical com-position of the copper trinkets he somehow obtained; he could only choose among the limited number of possibilities, but even then he was directed by criteria other than chemical composition or magnetic properties.

In some instances, people do change the surrounding

nature (i.e. they are not limited to a choice). In doing this, they are of course led by their brains: it certainly *is* cognitive behaviour but it may not be always intentional. Farmers of neolithic and bronze age Europe, for example, bred their cattle in such a way that the size considerably diminished during that period; yet, this effect was hardly their intention. There are many examples that fit into this class.

Elements of the artifactual record, however, were formed according to a plan which the producers had in their minds. No doubt, prehistoric farmers knew what angle the cutting edge of their axe should have, and how to decorate pottery destined for a particular occasion. It is often believed that prehistoric people had a list of attributes which their products should possess, and it is assumed that the resulting artifact was more or less 'composed' of these attributes, in a way similar to how a car is assembled in a factory.

This view of the process by which artifacts originate does not seem to reflect exactly how people worked in pre-industrial societies. It seems to me that artifacts were produced on the basis of learned procedures which I call *material algorithms*. If somebody tried to make a pot, he knew that it was necessary to take a piece of potter's clay, to throw at the centre of a wheel, etc. It was the sequence of necessary steps, not a list of necessary attributes, that the potter had in his mind. People who work on the basis of 'material algorithms' are often perplexed when asked to supply a list of properties: many of them originate outside the concentrated attention of the producers as a result of a routine application of the algorithm which proved to be successful to many preceding generations.

One might ask whether it would not be better to discard the 'artificial' way of description of contexts by means of entities and qualities and to introduce material algorithms in their place. Unfortunately, this seems to be impossible: archaeologists are able to observe the entities and the qualities but, for reasons of principle, cannot observe the 'algorithmic' procedures, which necessarily take place in the unobservable (past) time. By the way, it is one of the main goals of so-called experimental archaeology to rediscover the material algorithms: practical experience shows how difficult a task it is.

The problem of intentionality and of authentic 'prehistoric' concepts must be considered in the light of the preceding paragraphs. In many instances, at least, the archaeological concepts, derived from the records, may be superior to those based on the reports of the aborigines. This should not be a surprise: few people are willing to judge others on the basis of what they proclaim about themselves; why should archaeologists believe that the categorization devised by the producers is inherently better than their own?

4.2.7   The analysis of ecofacts and natural facts

If analysis in general cannot be performed without some measure of previous theoretical knowledge, then the analysis of ecofacts ought to be different from that of artifacts. The relevant theory (in the form of models) cannot be formulated by archaeologists alone, as they do not possess the specialized knowledge on the world of nature of which the ecofacts form a part. Natural scientists are needed to help in this task.

However, ecofacts are not entirely 'natural' objects as their properties were partly determined by human cultural behaviour. Thus, for example, the genetics of domestic animals must have been deeply influenced by the forms of breeding of the herds. As a result, natural scientists are also unable to work on the archaeological ecofacts in isolation, i.e. without the archaeologists. This creates a large field for cooperation.

Let us note that this type of cooperation is different from the role of natural scientists during the description of artifactual data. In the latter case it is assumed that the data are purely natural objects, while in the case of analysis of ecofacts it is recognized that the seemingly natural objects have properties brought about by human behaviour. It is two kinds of activities on two different levels of abstraction that cannot be directly compared.

The role of the archaeologist in selecting the ecofactual data usually consists in asking questions which the natural scientist transforms into the natural properties that could bear on the questions. The natural scientist would otherwise choose his own problems and on their basis he could derive his own attributes which might provide nothing of interest for the archaeologist. For example, the archaeologist may ask the zoologist whether there is any evidence for the winter feeding of domestic animals, in what season they were killed and at what age. These queries may lead the zoologist to look for observable attributes on animal bones to be able to determine the age at death and possibly the sex of domestic animals more accurately than is usual in his own discipline.

The natural scientist sometimes appears to be self-sustaining in asking archaeological questions but this is mostly because he derives them from archaeological literature, from what he has heard during various archaeological sessions, etc. Some of the archaeological questions, however, such as the absolute chronology, are so well known even to the general public that the nuclear scientist really does not need to be asked to devise a dating method. As far as I know, there was no archaeological incentive at the origin of most dating methods, including the development of radiocarbon dating.

There are several forms of cooperation between archaeologists and natural scientists in the field of ecofact analysis. In many of them, there is a one-way dependence of the former on the latter. This group includes, for example, chemistry and various branches of biology, where the problem is perhaps to determine the biological species contained in some archaeological sample. What is demanded is routine identification, which is usually unattractive for the natural scientist.

Another class of scientists, such as some types of physicists, are more interested in working for archaeologists, as the cooperation may involve some peculiar measuring problem which is not trivial and possibly not yet routinely applied. Many dating methods (e.g. thermoluminescence) belong to this category.

4.3   Analysis in the field

This chapter has so far not been interested in the question how the archaeological context to be analysed has in fact originated, whether by identification in the field or by specification based on records already at hand. The former case of obtaining contexts (archaeological excavations) opens certain questions that need not be considered in the latter case. In general, the problems of fieldwork are felt to be of prime importance by most archaeologists, especially in view of the fact that the discipline as a whole is often 'identified' with excavation (e.g. Hensel 1986). This is, of course, an unsatisfactory view: the quantity of the archaeological record is limited and it is certain that excavations will be much less frequent in the future; it is not impossible that one day there will be no further possibility of excavating because no archaeological contexts are left. I hope this rather grim perspective will not be realized, but it is certain that the vast majority of future archaeologists will have to work on the basis of finds excavated by preceding generations. In view of these facts, at least, archaeology cannot be identified with fieldwork.

The still untouched sites will be studied primarily by means of non-destructive methods of geophysical and geochemical prospecting. The prospecting methods used so far seem to be on a rather elementary level and their results are often unrewarding: the traditional archaeological excavation provides so much more that geophysical prospecting is usually used more for saving time and money than for saving the site. The results of some of the recent advances in this field, however, are promising and there is no reason why these methods should not attain the level of computer tomography common in contemporary medicine. Many archaeologists would then prefer them to traditional excavations.

The essence of excavations is the *isolation* of archaeological facts from their context, their transportation into a museum collection, and the documentation of what is usually called the contextual information. All this activity could be described simply by means of the analytical concepts introduced so far were it not for the fact that the excavation is also a powerful transformation of the archaeological record. As such, it dramatically reduces the information that survived from the past up to the present and, consequently, it should also be discussed from this point of view. If a context is obtained by specification, there are hardly any such problems (unless destructive analyses are used).

There is a principal difference between the two 'products' of an excavation: the finds and the documentation. While the former can repeatedly be studied using new lists of variables, the latter is a 'closed' piece of information. What has not been included in the description of a house in the field, and what has not been documented by a photograph or by a drawing, can rarely be added to the documentation later.

The naïve optimists among the traditional archaeologists not only believed that the number of finds was practically unlimited, they also assumed that their own field research did not miss any important information: all finds were believed to have been recovered and all the contextual information recorded. As we now know, this is not attainable for reasons of principle. Even sifting all the 'cultural' layers of a site, one loses the archaeological facts whose diameter is less than the meshes of the sieve; and it is known that some of the microscopic facts are very important (e.g. pollen grains). But what may be even worse is the loss of the contextual information resulting from the fact that the documentation of any excavation cannot record anything but a rather limited number of spatial relations.

For example, if a bronze age 'refuse' pit contains 1000 sherds on average and one settlement site consists of more than 1000 such pits, it is materially impossible to record the exact position of each of the sherds by means of methods which we now have at our disposal. Traditional archaeologists would probably say that the exact position of sherds is not important and it may well be the case. But who can swear to it, if so few have tried on the basis of an acceptable sample? Another example: no archaeologist of the middle of the twentieth century ever had the idea of measuring the faint radioactivity of the earth surrounding prehistoric pottery; yet this is now known to be important for thermoluminiscence dating. However, if a sample for the measurement is not taken during the excavations (and measured very soon), the relation between the amount of luminiscence in the sherd and the activity of the surrounding soil is lost forever.

The loss of contextual information resulting from archaeological excavations is tremendous. Information lost in this way can never be retrieved as the excavations completely destroy the original spatial arrangement of the finds; all things that are not recovered are also lost. Considering the situation from this point of view, it is necessary to admit that archaeologists belong among the most persistent destroyers of their own record.

To stop excavating may not be the best method of solving this problem. Field methods can only be developed on the basis of further excavations, as it is impossible to make a practical activity more precise by simply contemplating it. Moreover, the number of archaeological sites that are destroyed by non-archaeologists is still increasing in most parts of the world: rescue work is urgently needed to salvage at least something out of what would otherwise be lost completely. However, it is a highly responsible task to excavate sites that could lie intact in the earth for another millennium.

It is particularly disquieting that there are still a lot of general-purpose excavations whose necessity cannot be grounded otherwise than in a desire 'to see what is there' or to make a discovery. As the results of archaeological excavations are mostly uninteresting in themselves (i.e. if not analysed in their wider context), they often remain unpublished. Such unpublished general-purpose excavations are quite a problem in some countries as they often concentrate on a non-random selection of sites; their destroying effect can be considerable.

The New Archaeology has arrived with a requirement to excavate to test a previously established hypothesis. This corresponds to the overall task of any kind of analysis as discussed in this chapter: analysis always starts from a theory (or a model) expected to be confirmed or rejected by the context to be analysed. Most often, however, the theory is simply made more or less probable as a result of the application of the archaeological method, and this is also the case of the 'physical' analysis, which archaeological fieldwork is. It should be noted that even the 'general purpose' excavations in fact test a hypothesis – something like 'there is something unexpected in the earth' – and from time to time the result of the test is positive. What is unsatisfactory with this kind of 'testing' is that the starting hypothesis is rather abstract; the same results can be achieved by any fieldwork in general.

If the reason for new excavations were not the testing of

new theories, it would be incomprehensible why any new archaeological materials would be needed at all. The archaeological record in itself never asks questions: it is its theoretical aspect that brings in the uncertainties characterizing almost any fieldwork and usually leads to another field campaign. However, an archaeologist who denounces or neglects theory poses a limited number of questions (usually those ensuing from his unconscious paradigmatic standpoints) and therefore is less likely to discover anything unexpected. This is a clear paradox hidden in the quest for discoveries.

In general, what leads archaeologists to ever new excavations may not always be an attempt to discover something unexpected but rather to do their job better than the last time. For example, if a new theoretical model discloses that the height above the bottom of a grave pit at which grave goods are situated may be important (a structuring quality), a desire to excavate another cemetery of the same kind as formerly seems to be natural.

It is sometimes maintained that the requirement to 'test hypotheses' by means of excavations cannot be reconciled with the demand to give priority to rescue operations, but this is certainly not true. Salvage work can be adapted to this requirement although it is demanding on the organizational skills of the archaeologists concerned.

At the same time it should be realized that the endeavour to save ancient monuments goes too far in some instances. In many parts of the world outside the Antarctic, the surface of the Earth (and in part also the bottom of the sea) is almost continuously covered by remains of past human activity or, at least, it was possibly a constituent factor influencing the life of some past human community. Almost anything is a part of the archaeological record in this sense and possibly an important one: it is generally admitted that the present-day density of artifacts is not decisive.

The mould of an otherwise 'archaeologically sterile' modern field may contain a few flints as the only remains of neolithic occupation. The near-by peat-bog will never produce any finds but its layers may provide evidence for the medieval cultivation of fields in that region. The loam accumulated in the valley of a brook, with no artifacts at all, brings testimony to the possibly recurring deforestation of the vicinity in the iron age.

Archaeologists tend to protect any prehistoric settlement site and certainly every individual barrow as these constitute the national heritage; the other parts of the country, which may contain much more information about the past, are left 'unprotected' because there are no monuments. This is somewhat illogical but there is perhaps no other straightforward way to protect at least something. The situation cannot be solved by extending the protection by law to any possible piece of the archaeological record, as this would mean an almost complete petrification of the present landscape. Archaeologists should perhaps realize that they find themselves in the position of those who conserve the beautiful and the conspicuous at the expense of the (possibly) important.

Any future archaeological analysis will necessarily depend, at least in part, on what we have excavated in recent decades. In those regions of the world where the rate of destruction is high, it is generally accepted that all sites cannot be 'rescued'. Thus, archaeologists have to choose, deciding at the same time what will be destroyed completely or almost completely. Here again, the conspicuous sites are usually preferred.

When I did rescue work in Bohemia in the 1960s, some 80 per cent of the sites we excavated were settlements of two culture groups: Knovíz (late bronze age, total duration some 400 to 500 years) and early to middle La Tène (early iron age, duration some 350 years). The region had been densely and continuously inhabited since the beginning of the neolithic (sixth millennium BC) but certain periods of prehistory were not represented by more than a few sites, each including several features at most. The Knovíz storage pits, full of pottery sherds, were omnipresent and gratifying to excavate, but the work spent on them took perhaps too much of our time which could otherwise have been devoted to the search for the 'rare' periods and features not traditionally looked for in Central Europe (such as various forms of ditches).

This kind of bias cannot be removed by any random sampling unless we consider the amount of information that a particular site is able to furnish. To measure the information exactly is a rather complicated task, but in general it holds that phenomena whose probability of occurrence is small provide much information when they are examined. It is clear, on this basis, that one obtains a very small measure of information excavating the most frequent types of sites, especially if they are rich (i.e. if they bring a great quantity of little-differentiated facts).

In view of the fact that archaeological excavations are a kind of analysis and that analysis requires a theoretical model since its very beginning, it is deplorable that too often fieldwork is divorced from theoretical considerations. This results on the one hand in repeating observations which bring nothing particularly new (when the feed-back to theory is missing) and on the other hand in unproductive theorizing based on unnecessarily incomplete evidence.

4.4   Archaeological description

Once the analysis of an archaeological context is completed, it becomes possible to describe it. Description is basically the reproduction of relations between the units obtained in the course of the preceding phases of analysis. The process of description can be best expressed by means of set theoretical concepts such as mapping (cf. Neustupný 1973b).

There are many variants of archaeological descriptions. One possibility is to describe items by means of variables (this is often believed to be the only type of description). To express traits by means of variables, however, is another example of the six basic possibilities. It is mainly for this reason that the terminology of description cannot remain the same as that of the preceding phases of analysis.

The initial sets of units obtained by means of analysis of a context form the *archaeological space*. The archaeological space, which is always related to the needs of a concrete synthesis to follow, consists of a set of *objects* which are characterized by a whole family of sets of *descriptors*. The result of description will be referred to as the *descriptive system*. In a particular instance, the space of a prehistoric cemetery may consist of the set of its graves (objects) described by means of a set of descriptors such as the length of graves, the position of skeletons and the types of vessels found in the graves. The table containing the information as to which states of the descriptors characterize the individual graves of a particular cemetery will be called the descriptive system. The terminology chosen for this division of the archaeological method partly reflects some more or less analogical concepts of mathematics such as that of space and system.

4.4.1 Objects and descriptors

The object of an archaeological space can be selected among archaeological points, traits, items and variables. The same is true about the descriptors. The most usual set of objects is represented by a set of items, while the most common descriptors are variables. Such a space corresponds to what empiricists consider to be natural and it is, indeed, one of the most usual cases. Any other combination is equally possible, although perhaps less frequent. But a description of points (e.g. graves of females) by means of a set of variables is common, as well as the description of items (graves) by means of traits (e.g. types of vessels).

The difference between objects and descriptors is a relative one: what plays the role of an object in one particular space may be a descriptor in another context. Any object can be described by all the descriptors of the same space and vice versa, but it is not always possible to synthesize structures on the basis of such a description. The set of objects may be the same as the set of descriptors and, in fact, many important types of archaeological spaces have this form. It is the case of incidence or correlation matrices, for example.

The objects and/or the descriptors can be either empirical or classificatory. The *empirical objects/descriptors* are directly observable – consequently they consist either of items or of variables. The *classificatory objects/descriptors* are either points or traits; in other words, they are instances of structuring units. There is no reason whatsoever why the classificatory objects/descriptors should be excluded, especially considering the fact that their description occurs frequently. The archaeological space containing exclusively empirical objects/ descriptors is called empirical, while that containing at least one classificatory object/descriptor is termed classificatory.

Any archaeological space includes a single set of objects but may contain many sets of descriptors. The space consisting of more than one descriptor is called multidimensional; it is typical of modern archaeology which works it up by means of so-called multidimensional (or multivariate) methods. In contrast to this, traditional methodology, being unable to process multidimensional spaces, broke them down into a number of one-dimensional (univariate) cases, each of which was considered separately. In exceptional instances, however, pairs of descriptors (dimensions) were compared graphically (e.g. graphs showing the relation between the length and the width of flint blades); other methods of comparison of pairs of one-dimensional spaces were extremely rare (statistical tests).

The archaeological objects and descriptors can be either cardinal (with subdivisions), dichotomic or nominal. This typology, which has been discussed in more detail in connection with variables (but which is also valid for traits; cf. section 4.2.5 above), determines the methods with which the resulting space can be processed. If at least one of the descriptors is nominal, a number of very effective mathematical methods are prevented because the space is not (mathematically) linear.

4.4.2 *Descriptive systems*

One possible explication of the concept of a descriptive system has already been given: it is the result of description, of the assignment of individual states of descriptors to the objects (or to pairs of objects) of the particular archaeological space. There are, however, three kinds of descriptive systems, all of them subsets of the Cartesian product of the set of objects with the sets of descriptors. The first of them is described here, for convenience, as descriptive system M, the other two are termed descriptive systems R and F.

The *descriptive system M* fits more or less the concept of set-theoretical mapping. Let us consider the set of objects O and the set G of states of descriptor D (selected from the set of possible descriptors of the given archaeological space); a subset S of the Cartesian product O × G is called mapping if each element of the set O is represented only once in the ordered pairs of S. The descriptive system M is a set of such mappings of the set of objects into the states of each of the descriptors of the given space. This formulation (which is not strictly formalized) is put forward here to show that the concepts of set theory are applicable.

The concept of the descriptive system M can perhaps be explained more simply (but perhaps less accurately) in the following way: each object can be assigned just one value for each of its descriptors; this assignment is called mapping from the set of objects into the set of descriptor states; the descriptive system M is then defined as the set of objects, the set of descriptors with their states, and the set of all mappings from the set of objects to the sets of descriptor states.

The descriptive system M can also be expressed in the form of a matrix. The rows of the matrix are arranged in the same order as the corresponding objects, the columns are arranged in the same order as the corresponding descriptors. The cells of the matrix contain the values of the mapping. Thus, for example cell (5, 4) contains the value that corresponds to descriptor no. 4 of object no. 5. The matrix of the descriptive system is often manipulated without the corresponding headings of the rows and the columns; it should be kept in mind, however, that the headings are logically inseparable.

The cells of the descriptive matrix may contain real numbers (if the descriptor is cardinal), binary numbers (if it is dichotomic) or words/symbols (if the descriptor is nominal) and it may also be filled with 'missing values' which are no numbers. Neither the inclusion of non-numeric values, nor the close association of the rows and the columns with their headings correspond to the usual definition of a matrix in various fields of mathematics. However, such a descriptive matrix is in full accord with relational database forms which may contain both non-numeric characters and missing values, and where at least the headings of columns are usually obligatory. It seems likely that the requirements of practical descriptions have put sufficient pressure on the creators of the database software to design a scheme which is useful outside pure mathematics.

The *descriptive system R* reflects the mathematical concept of binary relations. In this case, the set of objects O is identical with the set of descriptors: this means that the set of descriptors is again O. As it has been explained in part 4.2.2 above, any relation between points, traits, data and attributes can be conceived as a subset of a Cartesian product (O × O in the case discussed in this paragraph). The relation can be represented by a square symmetrical matrix where both the rows and the columns correspond to the objects, and the cells are filled either with 1 (if the headings of the row and the column form an ordered pair which is an element of the relation) or with 0 (if it is not the case). To put it in other words, the number in cell (k, j) is zero unless the relation to be represented holds for the i-th and the j-th object (in that case it equals 1). This may be a useful representation of binary relations but, surprisingly, it is rarely found in archaeological writings.

The *descriptive system F* reflects the mathematical concept of function. It is a set of triples selected from the Cartesian product O × O × R (where R is the set of real numbers) such that each element of O × O is represented just once. It can be again represented by means of a square symmetrical matrix where both the rows and the columns correspond to individual elements of the same set of objects O, and the cells contain real numbers such as distances between pairs of graves, correlations between decoration motifs on pottery, or the number of common occurrences of two types in individual features of a settlement site. As descriptive systems of this type subsume all kinds of measures of similarities, distances, etc., they are of great importance in archaeology.

It is worth noting that all descriptive systems F can be derived by means of computation from more elementary descriptive systems M (i.e. mappings). Thus, the system containing Euclidean distances of individual features can be calculated from their coordinates. A correlation matrix, representing a descriptive system, can be conceived as a product of the matrix of a transformed descriptive system M by its transpose, etc. This is the reason why this type of descriptive system is called derived or *secondary* while the descriptive system M can be characterized as *primary*.

4.4.3   *The realization and storage of descriptive systems*

Traditional archaeology expressed its descriptions by means of what looked like the natural language. Most of the descriptive systems were rather concise in the sense that the number of descriptors was limited; it was a widespread habit not to mention many objects while stressing the exceptional ones. Also, the incompleteness of the systems was usually tremendous, because the descriptions were performed by the method of contrasts or remarks: if some of the variables were considered to be within the 'normal' range, they were not mentioned, only the 'unusual properties' were remarked upon. As 'normal' and 'usual' was not defined, the whole description was a highly subjective matter, and the individual objects were in fact rarely comparable.

Traditional archaeology, however, loved illustrations (whether line drawings or photographs) and the tendency to replace verbal description by means of figures is still considered to be highly laudable. This is not without reason: if the representation of finds and their spatial relations by means of figures is really good, it is possible to derive from it a fairly wide spectrum of information, for example on shape and decoration, and if exact scale is given a variety of metrical properties such as length, distance, etc. can also be extracted. Publications containing good illustrations may therefore remain useful for many decades: the figures can often be transformed into a fairly detailed descriptive system with few cells made useless by incompleteness. The disadvantage of figures is that even the best of them reproduce but a limited set of attributes; with photographs, the objects are frequently deformed by an inappropriate angle or by a cheap lens. With many drawings even those details that are depicted are frequently too generalized, and much detailed information is left out altogether.

It is not by chance that archaeologists working within the typological paradigm put excessive emphasis on illustrations which expressed more or less reliably just those groups of variables that were believed to be the most valuable for the paradigm (e.g. shape and decoration). They also satisfied the requirement of empiricism to present an 'objective' description uninfluenced by previous theories. However, the figures did not constitute concepts, so that any further work with them often remained on an 'impressionistic' level. If any higher level were to be reached, the figures must have been turned into objects and descriptors formulated as abstract concepts, or this goal must have been attained without the intermediate link of the illustrations; thus, verbal description could not be avoided anyway.

The foregoing paragraphs are not to say that illustrations form an unnecessary part of archaeological publications. I do maintain, however, that their role is not description. Points, traits, items and variables are abstract notions which cannot be properly expressed by means of drawings or photographs; the use of numbers and/or verbal constructs, accompanied by formal definitions, is unavoidable (Malmer 1962).

As we have already learned, descriptive systems can be represented by matrices with columns and line headings. This is the usual form in which descriptions are published in methodologically orientated present-day archaeology. This form of publication is frequently preferred to a narrative, although the latter is, of course, acceptable. However, the narrative mode of description may be subject to omissions (it supports the tendency to a description 'by contrast') and, for the purpose of further treatment, it must usually be turned into a matrix anyway. Moreover, the matrix form of descriptive system can be most easily transformed into a relational database for which there are many programs for modern personal computers.

Some archaeologists believe that it is not necessary to publish extensive databases in the printed form, and there are good reasons for using something like present-day computer discs for this purpose. Most modern authors are still reluctant to admit that paper may not always be the best medium of scientific communication. In many of the early civilizations, however, knowledge was not spread by writing but by memorizing texts; so the idea that we may have another phase of science before us, based on carriers of information other than paper, should not be astonishing. But it is really difficult to make forecasts in the age of such quickly changing possibilities.

Anyway, it is unlikely that the usual publication on paper of a database consisting of several thousand objects and originating automatically would ever be rational, if such a database cannot be handled otherwise than by means of a computer. It is likely, however, that extensive descriptive systems of that kind will be very important in the future.

5

Archaeological synthesis

Analysis, conceived in terms of the preceding chapter, is certainly not the end-product of scientific endeavour. It decomposes the archaeological reality into parts (units) which must be put together again, if something meaningful is to be produced at the end. The mental recomposition of reality is called synthesis, and the products of synthesis are (archaeological) structures.

5.1 The concept of archaeological structure

The concept of archaeological structure is, in fact, quite simple to understand in its generality The term denotes any *order, regularity, pattern or law of archaeological relevance contained in an archaeological context.* Archaeological structures can be seen from two angles: one of them is the order itself, its abstract aspect. Examples of structures approached from this point of view are unspecified types, culture groups, phases, tool kits, etc.

The second possible use of the term 'structure' is particularizing: it is *any particular kind of order in any particular context.* In this respect it resembles the concept of the 'particular' culture frequently discussed in traditional methodology (cf. archaeological cultures such as Michelsberg, Linear Pottery, Sesklo, etc.). Incidentally, the latter named cultures are also examples of archaeological structures in this particular aspect. Other examples are as follows: the early phase of Bell Beaker pottery, male equipment of the Corded Ware culture, individual types of La Tène fibulae, etc. The number of all possible archaeological structures, if conceived this way, is enormous and they cannot be enumerated in advance of their synthesis.

The generation of structures contained in a context is performed on the basis of its descriptive system. The archaeological space used in the process of the synthesis of structures determines its results: if the space is badly designed, i.e. if the context is improperly analysed, no method can generate a representative set of valid structures on its basis.

'Structure' belongs among overloaded words. One of its meanings in archaeology has already been discussed (section 1.5) and the sense in which I am going to use it in this chapter is similar or even identical to that presented earlier. However, to be sure that the term is understood properly, I add the adjective 'archaeological' where needed. Structure in general is the internal order of things, and 'archaeological structures' are both the general and particular regularities contained in the archaeological record as generated on the basis of its analysis.

It is always difficult to give a formal definition of concepts as general as 'structure'. I have presented two of them in the preceding paragraphs (together with some examples) but I feel that these definitions are not entirely correct as they include words whose meaning would also require comment: it is questionable whether 'order', 'regularity', 'pattern' or 'law' are clearer in their contents than the 'structure' which they are supposed to define. Anyway, the definition at least displays an overall idea of how the concepts are used in the present book and the following passage may help the idea become more concrete.

Archaeological structure is an *abstraction* contained in the record. In consequence of this, it is not identical with any of its concrete constituents (artifacts, ecofacts, etc.). Traditional archaeology often suggested, for example, that its types are groups of artifacts and/or that they can be represented by any artifact which 'belongs' to the respective group: this is the theoretical basis for figures headed 'Pottery types of culture X'. Looking at such figures, however, we discern individual pots but no types; each of the pots may be an archaeological point but certainly not the structure of the pots.

Any archaeological structure is *formal* in the sense that there is no need to consider its meaning during its generation. Once there is a descriptive system (which, of course, cannot originate without meaningful models) the meaning may be forgotten, to be resuscitated only during the next methodological step of interpretation. In the step of synthesis, however, it is exclusively the oppositions within the descriptive system that matter. Being formal, archaeological structures are at the same time *static*. True, they are reflections of some formerly living structures but, at the same time, they cannot be identified with them. The 'language' of the archaeological record, as represented by a set of archaeological structures contained in a context, does not 'express' any function, meaning and significance, and it also lacks any time coordinate; it is therefore questionable whether it can be described as a language at all.

When I stress the objective existence of archaeological structures, I step into an argument with empirically orientated archaeologists, who believe that structures (if there are any) are mere groups of finds or groups of the properties of finds. Developing the empiricist standpoint, consequently, the next logical step would be to assume that it is archaeologists who impose the structure on the 'data' (as somebody has to create the structure if it is not contained in the individual facts). The Münsingen fibula need not be conceived, according to these views, as an abstract entity; it is assumed to be a set of concrete finds which share certain characteristics selected by us, archaeologists. This way of thinking reflects one of the most basic attitudes towards the world around us connected with the question whether the world contains any pattern at all or whether it is man who imposes his subjective patterns upon reality. Without answering this admittedly difficult question, let us note that the empiricists, who mostly believe themselves to be materialists, end up with a very subjective variety of idealism. At the same time, if order is put into the archaeological record by archaeologists, it clearly does not reflect anything of the past. If this were to be accepted, what sense would there be in studying archaeology at all?

Archaeological structures appear as abstract objects of the descriptive system mapped into a set of its descriptors. A bell beaker is *a beaker with a bell-shaped body and a flaring neck, often decorated on both the neck and body by horizontal zones; sometimes it has a strap handle*. The accuracy of this 'definition' is rather low because it works outside a previously defined context and no space of objects and descriptors has been specified in advance. Also, the definition uses quantifiers such as 'often' and 'sometimes', which have a rather subjective meaning. However, if these 'deficiencies' were removed, the definition could be accepted.

The chapter on analysis has shown how archaeologists try to select the entities and qualities that are structuring, i.e. to include into their descriptive systems objects and descriptors which can be utilized to generate structures; the selection is achieved by means of models. However, the process of reducing points and traits to items and variables results in the situation that all the elements of the descriptive system need not be structuring. One of the tasks of the synthesis of structures is just to exclude such non-structuring elements. This can be done in two ways, which more or less reflect the historical development of archaeology.

One way is to exclude the descriptors that are not 100 per cent characteristic for the structure. This usually results in a fairly limited number of descriptors characterizing the structure; each of the descriptors, however, is both sufficient and necessary for the delimitation of the structure. Structures of this kind are usually called *monothetic* and they were characteristic of traditional archaeology. Not infrequently, a type of fibula was defined by a single variable, and there were rarely more than a few of them. This is understandable, as any larger number of descriptors (all of which must be present *at the same time*) would not work: each type of fibula would then consist of a few pieces only.

It was felt, however, that this procedure was unsatisfactory: an amphora, for example, might have three handles instead of two but still be almost identical to those with two handles. Should it be excluded from the class of amphorae because of the one handle in excess? This quite common situation was, of course, incompatible with the institution of monothetic structures; if the number of classes were to be kept in reasonable limits, the only solution was to accept exceptions which, in the absence of quantitative measures, quote often led to subjective decisions.

A satisfactory solution had to wait until the spread of mathematical methods, which brought the possibility of measuring the degree to which the individual descriptors had been characteristic for the structure to be defined. Such a structure was named *polythetic* (Clarke 1968); none of its descriptors were either necessary or sufficient for the delimitation of the structure as a whole. This does not mean, however, that any descriptor would be structuring in relation to any structure, but the number of descriptors allowed to characterize a structure greatly increased. Thus, the information contained in the descriptive systems could be used more effectively than within traditional methodology.

The fact that the synthesis of structures excludes a descriptor as non-structuring does not yet mean that it is unimportant. For example, a typological classification of pottery may exclude the 'thickness of walls' as non-structuring. It is well known that the thickness is functionally very significant, so it may perhaps stand out within a descriptive system aimed at the classification of functional classes of pottery. The variable 'fired clay' would never appear significant in synthesizing descriptive systems of pottery (if any pottery is made of fired clay, this descriptor does not oppose any other descriptor): however, it contrasts pottery with metal artifacts and, as a matter of fact, it cannot be structuring in an environment where everything is of clay.

The archaeological structure has been defined as any order, regularity, etc. *of archaeological relevance*. This specification is necessary because of the fact that the archaeological record consists of elements that are natural things and, consequently, they usually have their non-archaeological structures as well. 'Archaeological relevance', however, is a concept relative to the current state of research and the particular questions asked. The chemical composition of ancient potter's clay was not considered to be of archaeological relevance for many decades, and may still be non-relevant in many circumstances; yet, it has always been of (possible) interest for geochemistry, as the composition of clay is one of its 'structures'. In principle, any structure contained in any kind of record (including ecofacts and natural facts) may become an archaeological structure.

5.2   The traditional search for structures

Until quite recently archaeologists did not use the *term* 'structure' and even today its use is not frequent. Yet they did use what I call structures (types, culture groups, chronological phases, etc.), and they generated lots of 'particular' structures. It must be admitted that they were highly successful in these activities in spite of the fact that they knew next to nothing about the various mathematical algorithms that have been introduced into archaeology since the sixties. It is deplorable that the procedures which led the archaeologists of past generations to their remarkable accomplishments have rarely become the object of careful investigation (but cf. Gardin 1979). The two traditional algorithms, described in some detail in the following paragraphs, represent no more than a selection of what seem to me to be the most common methodological procedures.

The substance of the first method, a typically *exploratory* one, was a stepwise search for 'correlations' within a context whose descriptive system was not 'fixed' (i.e. it was open to sequential changes). The initial step was the visual representation of the context to be worked upon. This was usually done in the form of drawings or photographs, because the finds may have been deposited in several museums and it would be difficult to manipulate the material objects themselves. It should be remembered, however, that drawings were also used because they usually sufficed for the solution of questions posed within the framework of the typological paradigm.

Next came a repeated inspection of the figures together with experimental probing of all the possible and impossible descriptions. The archaeologist usually knew which descriptors had previously proved to be successful in similar circumstances. What variability is there in the formation of bases in the case of prehistoric pottery? Is the transition between bodies and necks sharp? What is the frequency of the incised decoration in relation to the next most frequent decorative technique? Through the interaction of his observations of the context and his ponderings on the model, the archaeologist derived his descriptive system in spite of the fact that he was probably ignorant of the concepts of both the descriptive system and the model. No doubt he was convinced that he described his finds entirely 'objectively', i.e. without the use of 'preconceived' ideas.

If the (unexpressed) model of the variability of a ceramic context were temporal changes, it seemed natural to select descriptors such as the shape of pots, the formation of their rims, the decorative motifs, the technique of decoration, etc. Archaeologists knew in advance that it was these descriptors that most usually measured time. The search for 'correlations' between the elements of the descriptive system just elaborated was almost instantaneous; if no pronounced correlation was found, the set of descriptors was partly changed and another iteration of the search started. The intertwining of analysis and synthesis was quite common, being one of the very efficient procedures of the traditional method (by the way, as far as I know, it has not yet been programmed for a computer).

'Correlations' were most often measured intuitively or by means of common occurrences in the best case. There was usually no discussion of their statistical significance simply because this was not considered to be a serious problem; yet the method worked. If the sharp body profile of beakers 'correlated' with the presence of strap handles, while the S-profile was always connected with beakers without handles, the archaeologist could hope to have hit upon a chronological division (chronology was, of course, believed to be the principal cause of variation). It was now necessary to take each of the two beaker groups separately and to try to determine whether there were any further descriptors limited to only one of the groups. It could also be investigated whether other classes of pottery (or possibly other classes of artifacts) did not correlate with the two types of beakers. It was usually in this way that the chronological system of a context slowly came into being.

There were many obstacles such as the fact that the observed correlations were hardly ever 100 per cent certain; if there was an S-profile beaker with a handle (to use the preceding example), the archaeologist had to decide whether it disproved his original classification, or whether it was just an exception (possibly a phase of transition) which needed no special consideration. It may have been for these 'unclean' correlations (with values less than 1) that the first generation of archaeologists, who still had comparatively few finds at their disposal (and, consequently, were aware of few exceptions), often arrived at classifications superior to those preferred later, when the great quantity of finds resulted in almost everything 'correlating' with everything else.

What we have just analysed is a typical exploratory or inductive procedure. I shall mention at least one further algorithm of traditional archaeology, with which the deductive aspect is more pronounced. It is the *method of confirmation*, which starts from some already known division. For example, the problem is as follows: assuming that our context, a cemetery, consisted of graves of both men and women, is it possible to decide whether the two groups of graves differ? If this question is responded to in the affirmative, the presence of two structures will be assumed (the male and the female grave equipment).

The problem of delimiting these structures is comparatively easy to solve if there is some kind of independent evidence which enables the archaeologist to decide whether the skeleton in a particular grave is male or female. This information can be supplied by physical anthropologists as the so-called external evidence. In cases other than our example, the division can be assumed on the basis of previous knowledge (or just tried haphazardly) and subsequently tested. The procedure itself is straightforward: one artifact after another is taken and inspected for its occurrence with either a male or a female skeleton. If an artifact type occurs indiscriminately with both the genders, it is dropped; if it appears exclusively with one of them, it becomes a descriptor of one of the two possible structures.

Here again, serious complications arise, if statistics is not used. The picture happens to be clear only as long as the number of graves is small; once it grows, usually no type of artifact turns out *exclusively* in the graves of one of the genders. It is then necessary either to accept the explanation that the archaeologist is facing exceptions, or to devise subsidiary rules and/or *ad hoc* explanations to save the expected picture.

The traditional methods of synthesizing structures are certainly sophisticated. Their great advantage over computerized procedures is in their flexibility and the ability to develop and use models for improving the descriptions in virtually any phase of the method. Their disadvantages are as follows: the inability to express the 'correlations' quantitatively and, consequently, the inability to assess the probability that the obtained configuration is random; the inability to study more than one pair of 'correlations' at a time. Also, traditional methods are unable to handle more than several hundred objects and more than the interrelation of a few descriptors at a time. What should not be overlooked is the fact that the successful use of traditional methodology was often reserved to those representatives of our discipline who had a developed 'typological feeling', irrespective of whether they were also creative in other respects.

5.3   The mathematical approach to structures

If mathematics is the general theory of structures, as observed in section 1.6, it should be possible to exploit it for the task of structure synthesis. This is tempting not only for theoretical reasons, but also in view of the fact that most mathematical methods attempted so far in archaeology are aimed at the search for structures.

It is not possible to unite all the aspects of the synthesis of structures by means of a single mathematical theory. In addition to the fact that there may be several such theories, the main obstacle to this is the character of archaeological facts, which in part consist of 'nominal' and/or incomplete data and, consequently, cannot be modelled by so-called linear (vector) space. However, no mathematical theory has so far been developed which includes both linear and non-linear cases on an equal basis.

The preceding paragraph uses the term 'linear' which needs some explanation. This term is often understood to denote something very elementary, more or less excluding any more complicated cases. This view is, no doubt, based on the evocation of school mathematics where linear equations were the most simple kind of equation followed by a series of more sophisticated concepts: quadratic and even higher-order equations, to say nothing of those containing logarithms or trigonometric functions. The linearity of algebraic spaces, however, has another meaning: it is defined by means of a set of axioms that convey a rather general notion. (These axioms will be discussed in more detail in section 5.3.3.)

While it is somewhat complicated to explain in the framework of these paragraphs what linearity of a space means, it is easier to recognize at least some of the cases of non-linearity. As in most of the applications used so far in archaeology the axioms of linear space include multiplication by real numbers, the elements of the space must again consist of real numbers for the result of the multiplication to be defined. The states of nominal descriptors are not real numbers and, therefore, the inclusion of a single nominal variable into an archaeological space makes it non-linear. The same situation occurs in the case of 'false zeros' (cf. chapter 4) and, of course, of missing values.

Elements of linear space can be scalars ('simple numbers') but most often they are vectors. A vecor is a column of real numbers (for the purpose of saving space in publications it is sometimes written in a line with commas as separators).

$$x = \begin{vmatrix} 5.4 \\ 9.2 \\ 7.0 \end{vmatrix}$$

$x' = (5.4, 9.2, 7.0)$
[x' is also called the *transpose* of x]

Thus, vectors are 'somewhat complicated' mathematical objects. Let us assume that we write down a series of numbers expressing the length of axes (of an archaeological context) into a column; what we get, is clearly a vector. Writing several columns (which may express other measurements taken on the same set of axes), next to each other we get a matrix identical with the matrix of the descriptive system of our previous example:

	(length)	(width)	(thickness)	(weight)
(axe 1)	98	27	19	90
(axe 2)	105	46	22	170
(axe 3)	105	44	16	140
(axe 4)	95	36	11	90

It is clear from the example that descriptive systems of many archaeological contexts can be conceived as linear vector spaces. This is the basis of many effective algorithms for the generation of archaeological structures.

There are two major groups of mathematical methods used in connection with the generation of archaeological structures. The first group encompasses *exploratory* procedures, which rely more or less on inductive philosophy. Their starting point is an empirically derived descriptive system where the role of objects and descriptors is played by items, variables, points and traits; the exploratory methods try to find out whether there is any structure in such a descriptive system (the other possibility is that descriptors are assigned to objects randomly). The nature of these exploratory methods is mostly non-statistical and they will be described in more detail in sections 5.3.3 (the linear case) and 5.3.5 (the nonlinear case). The so-called (exploratory) factor analysis and various clustering methods are examples of this group.

The second group includes *confirmatory* procedures. They are often believed to yield more secure results, mainly because of their close links with statistics. However, they assume that much is known in advance: the archaeological structure must, in fact, be supposed before the methods are applied. Thus, they are unable to discover new, unknown structures, although they are able to confirm the concrete shape of those already set up. Moreover, most of the procedures used so far in archaeology require the acceptance of a restrictive hypothesis on a particular statistical distribution of the values of descriptors. A typical example of this group is the so-called discriminant analysis; more details can be found in section 5.3.4.

5.3.1   Geometrical representation of structures

Before considering the mathematical methods of structure generation I shall introduce the representation of archaeological structures by means of geometrical concepts. Mathematicians would probably use the word 'interpretation' instead of 'representation' but the former term is too often used by archaeologists as a synonym for explanation, which is, of course, a completely different notion.

The objects of a descriptive system can be conceived as points in a space whose dimensions are the descriptors of the objects. This empirical space is identical with *archaeological space* as introduced in section 4.4. It is easy to imagine such points if the number of dimensions is 1, 2 or 3 and it may not be very difficult to go over to more than three dimensions on the basis of rational considerations.

First, let us consider a two-dimensional space, i.e. a plane. Its axes will measure some archeological descriptor, e.g. a variable whose values are real numbers. As an example we may take geographical coordinates of individual prehistoric sites of a region (the position of each site will be determined by two coordinates, i.e. by a vector consisting of two elements). Some of the points of the plane (which will be called 'significant' or 'selected' points) may be chosen to represent the sites of our example. The 'selected' points may be distributed randomly over the plane, but this is, of course, unlikely. There are three types of possible non-random distributions of points in a plane:

(1) regular, which occurs if the selected points lie at the intersections of lines of a more or less regular network (strictly speaking, the lines of the network need not be distributed regularly but according to some non-random rule);
(2) on a straight line or on a curve, closed or open;
(3) clustering around a point or around a line.

These types of distribution can combine among themselves and with random distributions. Thus, for example, the points may form an arc (a non-random configuration), but the distances between any two neighbouring points may be random.

Prehistoric sites may be distributed according to any of the non-random principles or randomly. The most usual distribution will be (approximately) regular; in such a case it is often possible to define a network of sites by means of a more or less rectangular grid. Quite often, the sites will follow a line, especially if they lie on the banks of a river. Alternatively, they can cluster around some central site or on the shores of a lake. There are many combinations: sites can either be distributed randomly in clusters, or their density may increase non-randomly towards a particular point. It is sometimes rather difficult to decide whether a particular configuration of sites is random or not.

In another example, let us retain two dimensions but let us assume that they represent the length and width of stone axes. The most usual result will be points (i.e. axes) clustering around a straight line. The density of the points will probably increase towards a point (not necessarily 'selected'), which marks the average of the length and width. If there were two types of axes differing by their dimensions, there would be two different clusters, each with its own average point.

Now, the last mentioned case is important. Each of the clusters of points represents a 'type' of stone axe. In other words, it represents an archaeological structure. The structure, however, is identical neither with the set of clustering points (as there are certainly many other specimens of the type which are not represented by any point in the plot), nor with the average point. It is an abstract entity, which produces on the one hand the cluster and on the other hand the average.

But let us extend our example to three dimensions by including the angle of the cutting edge among the descriptors. The resulting descriptive system can, of course, be represented by Euclidean three-dimensional space, and the possibly resulting clusters will again represent some archaeological structures (types of stone axes). This can still be imagined and represented by a three-dimensional model though not easily drawn (as any drawing is necessarily a two-dimensional representation).

The addition of further descriptors, however, will create a multidimensional space, which can be neither imagined nor drawn (not even represented by a physical model), but which *can* be easily comprehended. By adding, for example, the width of the blade and the width of the butt, we obtain a five-dimensional archaeological space. Each of the axes will now be represented by a point in the five-dimensional geometrical space (characterized by five coordinates; these coordinates, of course, will constitute a vector). It is obvious that the points may again cluster, this time in five dimensions. If there was a transition from a cluster in two dimensions to the case of three dimensions, there is no reason why there should not be a similar transition to a cluster in five or more dimensions. In instances like ours it is quite easy to find clusters as, for example, the calculation of distances in a five-dimensional space is fairly simple (cf. section 5.3.3).

Let us assume that the number of clusters will not grow, so there will be two clusters in the five empirical dimensions. As we have already seen, this means two structures. The structures will most probably be polythetic, although all the descriptors may not be significantly tied to both structures. In such a case, however, it is unnecessary to represent the axes in a five-dimensional space as two dimensions would be sufficient.

By going from the five empirical dimensions to the two abstract dimensions expressing the two structures, *we accomplish a major shift from observed phenomena to the world of structures.* The two new dimensions, each of them 'composed' of several descriptors, are usually called 'latent' dimensions. It is quite easy to find them by means of a computer, at least in the case of linear vector spaces. The latent dimensions are archaeological structures.

I shall not go into further details of the geometrical representation of descriptive systems and structures. In many actual applications all the questions may be far more complicated. Each descriptor can characterize several latent dimensions which implies that the multidimensional clusters overlap, and each object can also belong to several clusters. These interrelations are so complicated that any attempt at a visual imagination of such real situations becomes a burden. Geometrical representation is good for a quick apprehension of some of the basic concepts on the basis of quite simple examples.

5.3.2   *Structuring pairs*

Let us first investigate how it can be recognized whether two descriptors contained in one descriptive system belong to one archaeological structure or not. In the light of the preceding paragraphs it can be expected that if they do, all the objects of the same cluster should possess similar or identical values for those descriptors. It is obvious that the dependence between two descriptors of the same descriptive system can be measured.

Many measures for this *dependence* or relationship have been proposed (cf. Clarke 1968, 531); they are supposed to measure distance, similarity, correlation, etc. It has become clear on the basis both of theoretical considerations and of practical experience that two of them are especially suitable for expressing structural relationships: the Euclidean distance and the simple (linear) correlation. Moreover, these two measures of dependence are closely related to each other (cf. section 5.3.3). This does not mean that the other 'coefficients' would be useless, especially when considering the non-linear case. The linear correlation coefficient, however, is easy to test for statistical significance, but the meaningfulness of such testing depends on whether the two descriptors have a rather narrowly defined (so-called normal) distribution of values.

It should be noted that the calculation of the correlation coefficient does not depend on the assumption of (statistical) normality: it can be objectively defined within linear algebra without any relation to statistics; the normality is needed only when it comes to testing. It is certainly just the sound algebraic basis of the coefficient that makes it superior to many other coefficients during the application of subsequent algebraic methods; its statistical properties play hardly any role in this 'success'.

Now, what does it mean that the correlation coefficient has high absolute values (something like 0.9 or −0.95) or the Euclidean distance is close to zero? Clearly, if the two descriptors that correlated in this way are taken as coordinates for the objects of the same descriptive system, the objects will form a cluster, which means that the two descriptors have structuring properties. For the correlation to attain a high absolute value it is obviously necessary that both the descriptors are structuring, as the correlation is a 'function' of two descriptors. Any such pair of highly correlated descriptors (or significantly correlated descriptors, if the condition of statistical normality is met) form a possible elementary structure which I shall call the *elementary pair*.

Elementary pairs are only *possible* structures for two reasons. First, they may prove to be only minor parts of a wider structure (which is frequently the case) and, second, it is not at all clear whether they are *archaeologically* relevant. If the two descriptors are variables of vessels such as the contents of aluminium and iron in the ceramic paste, they may well be highly correlated but this correlation may simply reflect the natural composition of clay without any relation to archaeological problems.

Elementary pairs, arranged in a matrix, are often the immediate starting point for more complicated mathematical algorithms of structure synthesis. For this purpose, however, complete matrices are usually used. Elementary pairs convey the elementary information, and in the beginnings of the use of mathematical methods in archaeology the manipulation with elementary pairs was common.

What is important with elementary pairs is the fact that they can be rigorously calculated even for pairs of states of two nominal variables. Let us consider two nominal variables such as *sex* (with states male/female/undetermined) and *form of grave pit* (states quadrangular/oval/unknown). These variables cannot be included in a space to be worked on by vector synthesis as this would cause non-linearity of the space. Not even decomposing the two variables into their states can help: the cell of the resulting matrix corresponding, for example, to the intersection of the (new) variables 'sex male'/'sex female' contains a 'false zero' and again causes non-linearity. However, there can be no objection against the calculation of correlations such as 'sex male'/'grave pit oval' or 'sex female'/ 'grave pit unknown'. The latter named elementary pairs carry much information which cannot be included in many matrices to be described in the next section of this chapter.

5.3.3   *Vector synthesis (structures in linear space)*

There are many procedures for obtaining archaeological structures by means of mathematical methods. They form several families, whose number can be expected to increase with further developments in this field. At the same time, no revolutionary changes are likely to appear in the near future, with the possible exception of the applications of fuzzy set theory.

I have chosen the name 'vector synthesis' for one of the families of mathematical methods that includes so-called factor analysis, principal component analysis, multidimensional scaling, correspondence analysis, etc. They are all based on some kind of *vector* as initial input and they *synthesize* structures (in spite of their names that imply a kind of analysis); all of them are non-statistical in the sense that they do not necessarily test statistical hypotheses and do not rely on a prescribed statistical distribution. Some of the concrete varieties of methods, however, have been formulated in such a way that they do belong to statistics. The mathematical basis of the various methods of vector synthesis is similar, although the numerical algorithms differ. They are typically exploratory: very little has to be presupposed about their results. Both the number of 'factors' to be derived and their concrete configuration is unknown in advance.

It is sometimes argued that mathematically orientated archaeologists *apply* some kind of algorithm to their finds without being able to explain why its results should be accepted. I shall try to show that at least a part of mathematics is contained in the archaeological record, and it is just for this reason that mathematical methods do work in archaeology. Moreover, the mathematical methods for the generation of structures represent a generalization of traditional methods used for the same purpose in the past (and, of course, quite frequently up to the present).

It has already been noted that the individual descriptors of a descriptive system can often be represented by means of vectors. The whole matrix of the descriptive system then represents a linear vector space. I shall now demonstrate that the individual axioms of the linear vector space can be interpreted in terms of archaeological concepts and their properties. In the following paragraphs, I shall use the symbols x, y, z for vectors and α, β for scalars (real numbers). M 1, M 2, etc. will denote the 'mathematical' statements, A 1, A 2, etc. their archaeological counterparts.

(M 1) For any linear vector space mathematicians defined addition of elements in the following way:

$$\text{if } x = \begin{vmatrix} x_1 \\ x_2 \\ \cdot \\ \cdot \\ \cdot \\ x_n \end{vmatrix} \quad \text{and } y = \begin{vmatrix} y_1 \\ y_2 \\ \cdot \\ \cdot \\ \cdot \\ y_n \end{vmatrix} \quad \text{then } x + y = \begin{vmatrix} x_1 + y_1 \\ x_2 + y_2 \\ \cdot \\ \cdot \\ \cdot \\ x_n + y_n \end{vmatrix}$$

The result $x + y$ belongs to the same linear vector space. The addition is commutative and associative, i.e. it holds

$$x + y = y + x \text{ and}$$
$$x + (y + z) = (x + y) + z.$$

If o is the so-called null element (a vector consisting of a column of zeros), then $x + o = x$. For each vector x there exists its inverse $-x$ such that $x - x = o$.

(M 2) For any element of a linear vector space there is defined scalar multiplication (i.e. multiplication of a vector by a real number) whose result again belongs to the same linear vector space:

$$\alpha x = \begin{vmatrix} \alpha x_1 \\ \alpha x_2 \\ \cdot \\ \cdot \\ \alpha x_n \end{vmatrix}$$

The following equations hold:

$$\alpha(x + y) = \alpha x + \alpha y$$
$$(\alpha + \beta)x = \alpha x + \beta x$$
$$\alpha(\beta x) = (\alpha\beta)x$$
$$1x = x.$$

(M 3) For some linear vector spaces mathematicians define another operation called the inner (or dot or scalar) product of two vectors:

$$(x, y) = (x_1 y_1 + x_2 y_2 + \ldots + x_n y_n).$$

The result of this operation is a scalar (a real number), not a vector. The operation satisfies a set of conditions.

The inner product makes it possible to introduce some important concepts:

(a) $+ \sqrt{(x, x)} = \|x\|$ is called the Euclidean norm or the length of x; by dividing every element of x by this norm, we get a *normalized vector* x whose lengths equals 1 ($x^N = x/\sqrt{(x, x)}$ and $(x^N, x^N) = 1$).

(b) $+ \sqrt{(x - y, x - y)} = \|x - y\|$ (i.e. the Euclidean norm of the difference of two vectors x and y) is, in fact, a general expression for the distance between the two vectors; it can easily be verified that the well-known distance between two points in a 'real' plane or in a 'real' three-dimensional space is a special case of this formula.

(c)   Let $x^N = (x - c_1)/\|x - c_1\|$ and $y^N = (y - c_2)/\|y - c_2\|$. c_1 and c_2 are vectors, each consisting of n identical elements called the average (value) of x and y respectively. x^N is clearly a vector of numbers from which there has been subtracted their average, and the resulting vector normalized by means of its Euclidean norm; y^N has the same meaning in respect of vector y. Now, the inner product (x^N, y^N) is the linear correlation coefficient of x and y. Because c_1 and c_2 can be simply understood as vectors with all elements identical (equal to a fixed value, not necessarily the average), it is obvious that the correlation coefficient need not be interpreted exclusively in statistical terms. It also becomes clear, why the Euclidean distance and the linear correlation coefficient do so well in vector synthesis: they are concepts directly derived by means of elementary operations on the vector space, while a lot of other coefficients do not possess this property.

(M 4) If vector x can be expressed as

$$x = \alpha y + \gamma z$$

(where α and γ are not zeros at the same time), it is said to be a *linear combination* of y and z. A vector can be a combination of more than two vectors. A set of vectors $x_1, x_2, x_3. \ldots .x_n$ is *linearly dependent* if it contains at least one vector that is a linear combination of others; if there is no such vector, the set is *linearly independent*. Orthogonality is a special case of independence: two vectors x and y are *orthogonal* if $(x, y) = 0$ (i.e. if their inner product is zero). For obvious reasons, if $(x, y) = 0$ then $(x^N, y^N) = 0$ and also $\sqrt{(x, y)} = 0$. Zero correlation is thus a special case of independence and (more strongly) of orthogonality.

If x^N and y^N are two vectors normalized by the Euclidean norm and if

$$(x^N, y^N) = 1$$

the vectors are completely (maximally) dependent; in circumstances where it is only the dependence that matters, one of the vectors can be replaced by the other. Thus, the inner product of two vectors is a simple measure of their dependence.

In the case of more than two vectors the task of verifying their independence is more laborious: in general, it is necessary to calculate all possible inner products to see whether some of them equal zero.

(M 5) A set of linearly independent vectors of a vector space is called its *base*; the base of a particular space is not unique, i.e. there is more than one base for each vector space. Some of the bases are orthogonal, which means that the inner product of any pair of vectors selected from the base equals zero. The orthonormal base is an even more specialized notion; it is an orthogonal base in which the length of all the vectors is equal to unity.

There are effective algorithms by means of which a base can be found for any vector space; these algorithms, however, require such an amount of calculations that they cannot be performed without a computer.

But let us now turn to the problem of what archaeological meaning can be linked with the mathematical theory explained so far. The fact, already stated, that at least a part of the archaeological descriptors can be compared to mathematical vectors is the basis of the following comparisons.

(A 1) Let us consider two archaeological descriptors x and y written in the form of vectors. Let x be the set of numbers expressing the frequency of five types of decoration of sherds found in subterranean house 18 of a prehistoric settlement

$$
x = \begin{vmatrix} 16 \\ 24 \\ 0 \\ 6 \\ 0 \end{vmatrix} \quad
y = \begin{vmatrix} 32 \\ 48 \\ 2 \\ 12 \\ 0 \end{vmatrix} \quad
x + y = \begin{vmatrix} 48 \\ 72 \\ 2 \\ 18 \\ 0 \end{vmatrix}
$$

site, and let y represent the same kind of numbers for house 20 of the same site. $x_1 = 16$ and $y_1 = 32$ may be the numbers of incised sherds found in houses 18 and 20, respectively; 24 and 48 may be the numbers of sherds with stamp decoration and so on. If there were only two houses at the site, the addition $x + y$ would be the sum of the finds (classed according to types of sherd decoration) from houses of the site. Thus, the sum has a sound archaeological meaning. An archaeological explanation can be found for almost any addition of two or more descriptors (vectors), the condition being, of course, that the objects of the two descriptors have the same labels, i.e. that they are identical. The 'archaeological addition' is both commutative and associative. The subtraction of descriptors occurs, for example, when archaeologists remove secondary intrusions from a complex. The 'null descriptor' represents an 'empty' entity or quality, i.e. such that does not appear with any of the objects.

(A 2) Let us characterize prehistoric axes by a series of variables

$$a = \begin{vmatrix} 12 \\ 7 \\ 3 \\ 1 \\ 6 \end{vmatrix} \quad b = \begin{vmatrix} 24 \\ 14 \\ 6 \\ 2 \\ 12 \end{vmatrix}$$

For example 12 ($= a_1$) means that the length of axe 'a' is 12 cm, 14 ($= b_2$) describes the blade width of axe 'b', etc. By mere inspection of the vectors, it becomes obvious that $b = 2a$, i.e. axe b is just twice as big as axe a. The product αa (for any real α) will represent the set of axes which differ by their dimensions but which have the same shape in terms of the descriptive system used (as all the ratios between any pair of measurements remain the same). Also the other axioms of the linear vector space from the group of scalar multiplication have an archaeological meaning: it can be easily verified, for example, that $0.5 (x + y) = 0.5x + 0.5y$ (the resulting vector may be a selection of pottery from houses 18 and 20 with only one half of items selected).

It should be noted, in connection with scalar multiplication, that the elements of descriptors must be considered to be real numbers even in cases when they are integer or rational numbers according to common sense (for example, if they mean 'the number of sherds'). Vectors composed of whole (integer) numbers multiplied by a real scalar give *real* vectors; thus, the results would not be the same as the original (integer) vector. Whole numbers are turned into real (or rational) numbers to enable even very primitive calculations: e.g. averages and percentages, and most statistics, would be completely impossible if this conversion were not accomplished as a matter of course. Similarly, if the descriptors are dichotomic, the binary numbers they contain must be turned into real numbers.

(A 3) Let us consider the following descriptive system:

	a (axe)	b (battle-axe)
grave 1	1	1
grave 2	0	1
grave 3	1	0
grave 4	1	0
grave 5	1	1

$$(a, b) = 1 \times 1 + 0 \times 1 + 1 \times 0 + 1 \times 0 + 1 \times 1 = 2$$

The inner product of vector a (axes) with vector b (battle-axes), when the presence and absence is expressed by 1 and 0 respectively, is equal to what archaeologists call the 'common occurrence' of axes and battle-axes. If the archaeological space has more than two (dichotomic) descriptors, the inner product (the common occurrence) can be calculated for any possible pair: the resulting matrix can also be understood as a product of the original binary matrix by its transpose.

It is obvious that distances and correlations between descriptors are numbers of the same kind as the widely used common occurrences. The properties of the former, however, are 'improved' by means of normalization and standardization.

It should be noted that the Euclidean norm $\sqrt{(x, x)}$, which is in fact equal to the sum of squared vector elements, is not the only possible norm. There are a lot of other numbers that fulfil the conditions laid down for mathematical norms. One of them is the simple sum of the vector elements (in the case that all of them are positive numbers). Normalizing vectors by means of such a norm (i.e. dividing every element by the sum of elements and subsequently multiplying the result by a factor of 100), one gets the usual percentages. Thus, the calculation of percentages is in fact a kind of normalization of vectors. This example makes it clear that it is very difficult, if not impossible, to do without the normalization of archaeological descriptors (i.e. vectors).

(A 4) Let us assume that descriptor y (maybe a settlement pit of a prehistoric site) contains as objects numbers that characterize the frequency of decoration elements in phase A while z contains the same numbers relative to phase B. If the site was inhabited for seventy years of phase A and thirty years of phase B, the frequency of decorative elements that archaeologists will find at the site may be

$$x = 0.70y + 0.30z.$$

This corresponds to the mathematical concept of linear combination.
Let

$$y = \begin{vmatrix} 21 \\ 0 \\ 0 \\ 79 \\ 0 \end{vmatrix} \quad z = \begin{vmatrix} 0 \\ 34 \\ 56 \\ 0 \\ 10 \end{vmatrix}$$

(the two vectors have been normalized by the simple sum of elements, i.e. they contain percentages). The inner product $(y, z) = 21 \times 0 + 0 \times 34 + 0 \times 56 + 79 \times 0 + 0 \times 10 = 0$; this means that the two descriptors are completely independent (orthogonal). The archaeological meaning of this statement is clear: the decorative elements that appear in y in any non-zero quantity are lacking entirely in z and vice versa. This is a rare case indeed, as y and z would normally contain few zeros if the sum of vector elements were not very small. This, however, does not matter in our examples.

When the vector space consists of vectors whose elements are non-negative throughout, the pattern of zeros and non-zeros of any pair of orthogonal vectors must be that as exemplified by the preceding vectors y and z. Once negative numbers are admitted, however, none of the orthogonal vectors need contain zeros.

Now, let us assume that the elements of y of the preceding example are counts of sherds with the respective types of decoration, and let us choose another pit among the features of the same settlement site:

$$g = \begin{vmatrix} 42 \\ 0 \\ 0 \\ 158 \\ 0 \end{vmatrix}$$

(z, g) is again zero but (y, g) is a non-zero number. However, normalizing both y and g by means of their Euclidean norms and taking the inner product one obtains

$$(y^N, g^N) = 1.$$

This means maximum (linear) dependence. Looking at the two descriptors, the reason becomes immediately obvious: the elements of g are exactly twice the elements of y (i.e. $g = 2y$). If (y^N, g^N) were neither zero nor unity, the two descriptors would be partly dependent, which is the most usual case in practical applications.

(A 5) Archaeological spaces usually consist of descriptors like x of paragraph (A 4): the descriptors are linear combinations of unknown orthogonal vectors y and z in the form like x = 0.70y + 0.30z (this is, of course, only one of the most simple examples). As stated in paragraph (M 5), it is always possible to find the orthogonal base of a vector space, which is exactly what is needed: a set of orthogonal vectors lying *at the base* of the space. The vectors of the orthogonal base are the independent constituents which determine the shape of the archaeological space; to put it in other words, the vectors of the base are connected with what has been described as structures of the space. The task of finding archaeological structures is closely related to the mathematical task of finding the orthogonal base of a vector space.

The paragraphs in section 5.3.4 below discuss an example of the application of vector synthesis to the context of a prehistoric cemetery. The method used in this instance is known as principal component analysis. It has been chosen for the purpose of exemplification because it is based almost exclusively on the properties of the linear vector space as explained above; at the same time it includes no assumptions about probabilistic distributions, etc.

Given a description system, the method proceeds to the computation of linear correlation coefficients. If the number of descriptors is n, the number of correlations is n × n. However, the matrix is symmetrical, and the diagonal elements equal to unity. Next, this matrix is subjected to a rather complicated mathematical algorithm, destined to determine its orthogonal base.

The algorithm results in the so-called latent vectors (or *eigenvectors*) and latent roots (or *eigenvalues*). The latent vectors $(x_1, x_2 \ldots x_n)$ are in fact orthonormal base vectors of the original correlation matrix; thus, they are mutually 'completely' independent and their lengths equal unity. The latent roots $(\lambda_1, \lambda_2 \ldots \lambda_n)$ are numbers that indicate how much variation of the correlation matrix is explained by the particular latent vector. Theoretically, the number of latent vectors equals the number of descriptors; the number of latent roots may be less (i.e. some of the latent roots can be zero). If the number of descriptors is n, then the values of all the latent vectors sum to n. Those who are acquainted with the bases of linear algebra may find it instructive to learn that the correlation matrix R can be expressed in the following way:

$$R = \lambda_1 x_1 x_1' + \lambda_2 x_2 x_2' + \ldots \lambda_n x_n x_n'$$

Each of the expressions $x_i x_i'$ (where x' is the transpose of x) is a matrix with n × n elements whose absolute value does not surpass 1. If each of such matrices is multiplied by the corresponding latent root (this implies simple multiplication of each of its elements by the latent root) and all the matrices are added, we get the original correlation matrix. This means, however, that the calculation of the latent roots and latent vectors is a kind of decomposition of the correlation matrix into a limited number of more simple matrices.

If λ_i is a small number, every number in the matrix $\lambda_i x_i x_i'$ will also be small and it will not add substantially to the correlation matrix. It is generally assumed that such latent root(s) and latent vector(s) are due to random oscillations in the values of the correlation coefficients and need not be considered. In consequence of this, the number of extracted 'factors' is usually much less than the number of rows and/or columns in the correlation matrix, because many latent roots of most 'archaeological' matrices are small as a rule.

The question of finding the 'right' number of factors may not be easy. In some cases, usually reproduced in textbooks on vector synthesis, there is a limited number of great latent roots forming a massive group followed by an unambiguous 'spring' to a series of very small roots. In many instances, however, the number of factors is difficult to determine because the latent roots diminish without any marked jump (this is more or less the case of our example in Table 5.4). Statisticians working in the field have devised methods for solving this problem automatically; but to achieve such a solution a number of assumptions have to be made and conditions fulfilled. Moreover, the results obtained in this way often do not conform to the logic of things.

The problem therefore remains delicate, and sometimes cannot be answered without trying several possible solutions and picking out the 'best' on the basis of non-mathematical judgement. There are also several empirically derived methods for the purpose: some authors recommend dropping the latent vectors whose latent roots are less than 1 and/or account for less than 5 per cent of the total variability of the matrix (i.e. 5 per cent from n). Fortunately, the consequences of failing to determine the number of factors exactly are not tragic.

Now, the latent vector elements each multiplied by a square root of its latent root are the famous *factor loadings*. (Terms like factor loading or factor score are, of course, derived from 'factor analysis', a particular form of which is designated in this book as vector synthesis, but they are applicable to the whole family of related methods.) For example, the sword of Table 5.5 has a factor loading of −0.185 in relation to factor 1 and a factor loading 0.839 in relation to factor 2 (cf. Table 5.6). These numbers express more or less how much the sword is correlated with factor 1 and factor 2, respectively (in more concrete words: the sword is probably 'insignificant' for factor 1 but highly significant for factor 2).

While the latent roots of a correlation matrix are always the same, the decomposition of the matrix into its base vectors does not have a unique solution. For example, the concrete values of latent vectors depend on the order of rows and columns in the correlation matrix. Thus, the factors (i.e. the latent vectors multiplied by the square root of their latent roots) must be adapted in such a way that this bias is removed. This is done by so-called rotation (most common, and the theoretically best defendable, is the 'Varimax' rotation) which does not change the most important properties of the factors. Unrotated factor loadings make sense only when displayed graphically, but the rotated factor loadings also make sense in numerical form.

The algorithm for the orthogonal rotation is derived from a set of postulates of the so-called simple structure. The principal idea is to achieve the maximum number of 'decomposable' sub-matrices within the factor matrix or, to put it more simply, to transform the elements of the individual factors in such a way that the maximum possible number of values of the factor loadings is either nearly 0 or nearly 1 while the distances (in the space determined by the factors) are conserved.

To show an example of what this theory looks like in practice, I have borrowed a small factor matrix from a textbook on factor analysis (Table 5.1). Although it originally meant something quite different, we shall give it an archaeological interpretation. Let us assume that the unrotated factors resulted from a correlation matrix among five types of personal ornaments. The first two latent roots were 2.87 and 1.80 respectively which leaves 0.33 for the remaining three roots, a pronounced spring indeed. This makes it clear that two factors are to be considered. The Varimax rotation changed the elements of the factor matrix, the 'factor loadings', substantially: as could be expected, at least seven out of the ten rotated factor loadings are very near to either 1 or 0 (only one, type 4 on factor 2, is in between). It should be noted that the sum of squares of factor loadings taken by columns (the latent roots) changed considerably following the rotation,

Table 5.1. *An example of the 'factor' matrix (unrotated principal factor solution).*

	unrotated factor loadings		rotated factor loadings		communalities
type 1	.58	.81	.02	.99	.99
type 2	.77	−.54	.94	−.01	.89
type 3	.67	.73	.14	.98	.98
type 4	.93	−.10	.82	.45	.88
type 5	.79	−.56	.97	−.01	.94
latent root	2.87	1.80	2.52	2.15	4.67

Source: Harman 1967, Tables 8.1 and 14.6.

while the sum of squares of the loadings taken by rows (the so-called communalities) did not change at all.

It is clear, on the basis of our simulated example, that there are two sets of personal ornaments: types no. 2, 4 and 5 (factor 1) belong to the first set, while types no. 1 and 3 (and to a certain degree also type 4) are characteristic of the second. The two sets (i.e. the two structures found) can now be interpreted in terms of non-formal concepts by means of the methods to be described in chapter 6.

Up to now we have found structures in the space of descriptors of the descriptive system. This raises the question whether anything similar can be discerned in the space of objects. The answer is in the affirmative: one can use the matrix of factor loadings and compute the required solution by means of so-called linear regression. The elements of the solution, called *factor scores*, are again arranged in a matrix with the number of rows equal to the number of objects and with each column corresponding to each factor. The factor scores, unlike the correlation coefficients and factor loadings, may be expressed by any real number. However, if the correlation matrix fulfils certain statistical conditions at least approximately, which is frequently the case, about two thirds of factor scores will lie in the interval from −1 to +1, and about 95 per cent of the scores in the interval from −2 to +2. Scores with absolute values greater than 3 will be very rare.

While the loadings characterize descriptors, the scores are numbers that characterize objects of the descriptive system: they express a 'measure' in which an object is 'typical' of a given factor. By calculating the factor scores we obtain what is often called a *dual solution*: the structures both in the space of the descriptors and in the space of the objects is found. While it is easy to come to such a dual solution in many branches of vector synthesis, it is often quite difficult to do so in the case of the clustering methods to be described in section 5.3.5.

5.3.4 An example of vector synthesis

The La Tène culture cemetery of Jenišův Újezd, the archaeological context used as the starting point of the example, was excavated at the end of the nineteenth century; in spite of this early date it is still the largest site of its kind in Bohemia (Waldhauser 1978). The excavators described 120 graves in sufficient detail to make it possible to include them in a description system to be run on a computer. The example presented in this chapter is but a small part of a more comprehensive investigation (E. Neustupný 1978). The other problems solved by means of 'mathematics' included, for example, the classification of iron age brooches from the site which reproduced, with a minimum of effort, the classification reached by traditional specialists after many years of intense studies.

Each of the 120 graves was mapped into a set of 24 descriptors, 17 of which were dichotomic (either present or absent in the grave), 3 were linear dimensions (such as length), and 4 were counts (number of fibulae, etc.). The full list of descriptors is presented here in Table 5.2. The selection of the descriptors was made after consultations with J. Waldhauser, an archaeologist who had worked in the field of La Tène archaeology by means of traditional methods for many years. The resulting choice was heavily affected by the exclusion, because of low counts, of other available descriptors felt to be of possible importance: for example, if some class of artifacts appeared only twice in the cemetery it could not be used as it might influence the results adversely. In such a situation almost everything found and/or recorded in the field in

Table 5.2. *Jenišův Újezd, list of descriptors.*

artifact	no. of graves containing the artifact or average value or sum of the artifacts
1. bronze fibula	22
2. iron fibula	69
3. bracelet, right hand	29
4. bracelet, left hand	41
5. armring, right arm	7
6. armring, left arm	16
7. anklet	17
8. girdle	32
9. sword	18
10. spearhead	15
11. shield	5
12. fibula, neck or breast	51
13. fibula, shoulder	32
14. lignite armring	9
15. remains of textile	30
16. remains of coffin	30
17. bracelet, type −4/4	9
18. grave length	206.88
19. grave width	74.48
20. skeleton length	158.19
21. no. of fibulae	139
22. no. of rings	141
23. no. of bronze artifacts	175
24. no. of iron artifacts	198

sufficient quantities was included. In consequence of the consultations with Waldhauser, the descriptive system contained some previous knowledge on the La Tène culture. An example of a few lines of the descriptive matrix is given in Table 5.3.

The descriptive matrix served as a basis for the computation of the matrix of linear correlation coefficients, which is not reproduced here. It consisted of numbers in the interval from −1.000 to +1.000. Next, this matrix of correlations was orthogonalized by means of the principal component procedure.

Table 5.3. *Jenišův Újezd, a part of the description matrix.*

1	2	3	4	5	6	7	8	9	10	11	12	13	14	15	16	17	18	19	20
21	22	23	24																

grave 1
| 1 | 0 | 0 | 0 | 0 | 0 | 1 | 1 | 0 | 0 | 0 | 0 | 0 | 0 | 0 | 0 | 0 | 200 | 80 | 144 |
| 1 | 3 | 4 | 1 | | | | | | | | | | | | | | | | |

grave 2
| 1 | 0 | 1 | 0 | 0 | 0 | 0 | 1 | 0 | 0 | 0 | 1 | 0 | 0 | 0 | 0 | 0 | 200 | 75 | 153 |
| 1 | 2 | 4 | 0 | | | | | | | | | | | | | | | | |

grave 3
| 0 | 0 | 0 | 0 | 0 | 0 | 0 | 0 | 0 | 0 | 0 | 0 | 0 | 0 | 0 | 0 | 0 | 200 | 75 | 149 |
| 0 | 0 | 0 | 0 | | | | | | | | | | | | | | | | |

grave 4
| 1 | 1 | 0 | 1 | 0 | 0 | 1 | 1 | 0 | 0 | 0 | 1 | 0 | 0 | 0 | 0 | 0 | 200 | 80 | 153 |
| 4 | 3 | 5 | 3 | | | | | | | | | | | | | | | | |

grave 5
| 1 | 1 | 1 | 1 | 0 | 1 | 1 | 1 | 0 | 0 | 0 | 2 | 0 | 0 | 0 | 0 | 0 | 200 | 75 | 149 |
| 2 | 5 | 7 | 3 | | | | | | | | | | | | | | | | |

grave 6
| 0 | 1 | 0 | 0 | 0 | 0 | 0 | 0 | 0 | 0 | 0 | 0 | 1 | 0 | 0 | 0 | 0 | 235 | 75 | 186 |
| 1 | 0 | 0 | 1 | | | | | | | | | | | | | | | | |

grave 7
| 0 | 1 | 0 | 0 | 0 | 0 | 0 | 0 | 0 | 0 | 0 | 2 | 0 | 0 | 0 | 0 | 0 | 200 | 75 | 158 |
| 1 | 0 | 0 | 1 | | | | | | | | | | | | | | | | |

grave 8
| 0 | 1 | 0 | 1 | 0 | 0 | 0 | 1 | 1 | 1 | 1 | 0 | 1 | 0 | 0 | 0 | 0 | 235 | 85 | 180 |
| 2 | 1 | 1 | 6 | | | | | | | | | | | | | | | | |

grave 9
| 0 | 0 | 0 | 0 | 0 | 0 | 0 | 0 | 0 | 0 | 0 | 0 | 0 | 0 | 0 | 0 | 1 | 0 | 200 | 75 | 151 |
| 0 | 1 | 1 | 0 | | | | | | | | | | | | | | | | |

grave 10
| 0 | 1 | 0 | 0 | 0 | 0 | 0 | 0 | 0 | 0 | 0 | 1 | 0 | 0 | 0 | 0 | 0 | 200 | 70 | 160 |
| 2 | 0 | 0 | 2 | | | | | | | | | | | | | | | | |

grave 11
| 0 | 0 | 1 | 1 | 1 | 1 | 0 | 0 | 0 | 0 | 0 | 0 | 0 | 0 | 0 | 1 | 1 | 135 | 45 | 104 |
| 0 | 4 | 2 | 2 | | | | | | | | | | | | | | | | |

grave 12
| 1 | 1 | 1 | 1 | 0 | 0 | 0 | 0 | 0 | 0 | 0 | 2 | 2 | 0 | 0 | 1 | 0 | 230 | 85 | 176 |
| 6 | 4 | 6 | 4 | | | | | | | | | | | | | | | | |

Table 5.4. *Jenišův Újezd, the first ten latent roots.*

	latent root	
1	5.958	▮▮
2	4.132	▮▮▮
3	1.972	▮▮▮▮▮▮▮▮▮▮▮▮▮▮▮▮▮▮▮
4	1.737	▮▮▮▮▮▮▮▮▮▮▮▮▮▮▮▮
5	1.574	▮▮▮▮▮▮▮▮▮▮▮▮▮▮▮
6	1.096	▮▮▮▮▮▮▮▮▮▮
7	1.092	▮▮▮▮▮▮▮▮▮▮
8	0.873	▮▮▮▮▮▮▮▮▮
9	0.808	▮▮▮▮▮▮▮▮
10	0.695	▮▮▮▮▮▮▮

In the case of Jenišův Újezd the first ten latent roots, arranged according to their values, have been assembled in Table 5.4. The first two latent roots are clearly dominant, but they explain only some 40 per cent of the variability contained in the correlation matrix (in a matrix like ours the sum of all latent roots equals the number of its rows); the share of factors 3 to 5 is still considerable. The remaining latent roots (i.e. 6th and the following) are either very close to 1 or less than 1 so that the addition of each of the factors they might represent to the total variability of the matrix is negligible. This led me to retain five factors in this particular case. The decision was strengthened by the fact that the fifth factor is the last that expresses more than 5 per cent of the total variation; this is another empirically derived criterion for the selection of the number of factors. It must be realized, however, that the five factors taken together do not make up more than 65 per cent of the total variability of the correlation matrix; if our choice of five factors is right, then a large amount of 'noise' in the matrix must be assumed. However, this may well correspond to reality considering the rather small number of graves.

Once the number of factors is determined, the rest of the algorithm runs without any archaeological intervention. The factors displayed in Tables 5.5 to 5.9 have been ordered according to the values of their factor loadings; the rows of 8s

Table 5.5. *Jenišův Újezd, loadings on factor 1.*

	Factor 1			
1.	no. of bronze artifacts	23.	0.913	88888888888888888888888888888888888888
2.	bronze fibula	1.	0.852	8888888888888888888888888888888888888
3.	no. of rings	22.	0.847	888888888888888888888888888888888888
4.	anklet	7.	0.781	8888888888888888888888888888888888
5.	bracelet, right hand	3.	0.714	88888888888888888888888888888888
6.	bracelet, left hand	4.	0.538	888888888888888888888888
7.	no. of fibulae	21.	0.529	88888888888888888888888
8.	fibula, neck/breast	12.	0.427	888888888888888888
9.	girdle	8.	0.397	8888888888888888
10.	armlet, left arm	6.	0.283	8888888888
11.	no. of iron artifacts	24.	0.242	888888888
12.	lignite	14.	0.176	8888888
13.	armlet, right arm	5.	0.169	888888
14.	textile	15.	0.114	8888
15.	grave length	18.	0.110	8888
16.	grave width	19.	0.087	888
17	bracelet, type −4/4	17.	0.080	888
18.	coffin	16.	0.075	88
19.	skeleton length	20.	0.062	88
20.	fibula, shoulder	13.	−0.009	8
21.	iron fibula	2.	−0.026	8
22.	shield	11.	−0.068	88
23.	spearhead	10.	−0.168	888888
24.	sword	9.	−0.185	8888888

Table 5.6. *Jenišův Újezd, loadings on factor 2.*

	Factor 2			
1.	spearhead	10.	0.867	888888888888888888888888888888888888888888
2.	sword	9.	0.839	88888888888888888888888888888888888888888
3.	shield	11.	0.691	8888888888888888888888888888888
4.	no. of iron artifacts	24.	0.641	8888888888888888888888888888
5.	girdle	8.	0.593	8888888888888888888888888
6.	textile	15.	0.542	888888888888888888888888
7.	grave length	18.	0.308	8888888888888
8.	skeleton length	20.	0.254	8888888888
9.	grave width	19.	0.250	888888888
10.	fibula, shoulder	13.	0.136	88888
11.	bronze fibula	1.	0.080	888
12.	no. of bronze artifacts	23.	0.071	88
13.	armlet, left arm	6.	0.015	8
14.	no. of fibulae	21.	0.007	8
15.	bracelet, type −4/4	17.	0.004	8
16.	coffin	16.	−0.010	8
17.	armlet, right arm	5.	−0.054	88
18.	anklet	7.	−0.058	88
19.	bracelet, right hand	3.	−0.059	88
20.	no. of rings	22.	−0.074	88
21.	bracelet, left hand	4.	−0.075	88
22.	lignite	14.	−0.092	888
23.	iron fibula	2.	−0.113	8888
24.	fibula, neck/breast	12.	−0.157	888888

Table 5.7. *Jenišův Újezd, loadings on factor 3.*

	Factor 3			
1.	iron fibula	2.	0.882	8888888888888888888888888888888888888
2.	no. of fibulae	21.	0.642	888888888888888888888888888
3.	fibula, shoulder	13.	0.621	88888888888888888888888888
4.	no. of iron artifacts	24.	0.614	88888888888888888888888888
5.	fibula, neck/breast	12.	0.428	8888888888888888888
6.	bracelet, left hand	4.	0.362	88888888888888
7.	grave width	19.	0.300	888888888888
8.	textile	15.	0.294	88888888888
9.	coffin	16.	0.186	8888888
10.	no. of rings	22.	0.131	88888
11.	grave length	18.	0.122	8888
12.	bracelet, right hand	3.	0.119	8888
13.	lignite	14.	0.117	8888
14.	bracelet, type −4/4	17.	0.109	8888
15.	no. of bronze artifacts	23.	0.094	888
16.	armlet, left arm	6.	0.076	888
17.	girdle	8.	0.056	88
18.	skeleton length	20.	0.052	88
19.	shield	11.	−0.038	8
20.	sword	9.	−0.059	88
21.	bronze fibula	1.	−0.059	88
22.	anklet	7.	−0.068	88
23.	armlet, right arm	5.	−0.095	888
24.	spearhead	10.	−0.098	888

express graphically the value of each loading. To derive a description of, say, factor 1 on the basis of Table 5.5 it is necessary to decide which factor loadings should be considered: it is obvious that the descriptors connected with the loadings that are close to zero cannot be significant (for example the remnants of a coffin in the case of factor 1). Similarly, as in the case of the number of factors, this problem is difficult to solve.

A part of the matrix of factor scores (obtained by means of the principal component method) can be found in Table 5.10. Comparing its numbers with those of Table 5.3 one can see that grave 8, which contained a sword, a spearhead and a shield, scores high on factor +2, a typically male factor. Grave 5 scores high on factor +1 in accordance with the fact that it contained lots of ring ornaments typical of female graves.

Each of the five factors characterizes one or two archaeological structures, which can be described as follows:

Factor 1:   The grave furniture is generally rich; most of the bronze artifacts of the cemetery were found in graves

Table 5.8. *Jenišův Újezd, loadings on factor 4.*

	Factor 4			
1.	lignite	14.	0.711	88888888888888888888888888888
2	coffin	16.	0.597	888888888888888888888888
3.	armlet, left arm	6.	0.594	888888888888888888888888
4.	armlet, right arm	5.	0.547	88888888888888888888888
5.	no. of rings	22.	0.402	8888888888888888
6.	fibula, shoulder	13.	0.334	8888888888888
7	no. of bronze artifacts	23.	0.242	888888888
8.	textile	15.	0.231	888888888
9.	anklet	7.	0.227	888888888
10.	grave width	19.	0.205	88888888
11.	bracelet, type −4/4	17.	0.180	8888888
12.	no. of fibulae	21.	0.174	888888
13.	grave length	18.	0.173	888888
14.	bracelet, right hand	3.	0.163	888888
15.	bronze fibula	1.	0.060	88
16.	no. of iron artifacts	24.	0.060	88
17.	girdle	8.	−0.020	8
18.	skeleton length	20.	−0.026	8
19.	spearhead	10.	−0.053	88
20.	shield	11.	−0.081	888
21.	iron fibula	2.	−0.092	888
22.	bracelet, left hand	4.	−0.098	888
23.	sword	9.	−0.119	8888
24.	fibula, neck/breast	12.	−0.427	88888888888888888

Table 5.9. *Jenišův Újezd, loadings on factor 5.*

	Factor 5			
1.	bracelet, type −4/4	17.	0.545	888888888888888888888888
2.	bracelet, left hand	4.	0.198	8888888
3.	armlet, left arm	6.	0.196	8888888
4.	bracelet, right hand	3.	0.170	888888
5.	no. of rings	22.	0.107	8888
6.	fibula, shoulder	13.	0.087	888
7.	armlet, right arm	5.	0.023	8
8.	shield	11.	−0.030	8
9	lignite	14.	−0.057	88
10.	no. of iron artifacts	24.	−0.084	888
11.	no. of bronze artifacts	23.	−0.097	888
12.	iron fibula	2.	−0.131	88888
13.	anklet	7.	−0.165	888888
14.	no. of fibulae	21.	−0.168	888888
15.	sword	9.	−0.182	8888888
16.	fibula, neck/breast	12.	−0.183	8888888
17.	spearhead	10.	−0.185	8888888
18.	bronze fibula	1.	−0.193	8888888
19.	girdle	8.	−0.202	88888888
20.	textile	15.	−0.236	888888888
21.	coffin	16.	−0.310	88888888888
22.	grave width	19.	−0.617	88888888888888888888888888888
23.	skeleton length	20.	−0.783	8888888888888888888888888888888888888
24.	grave length	18.	−0.811	88888888888888888888888888888888888888

Table 5.10. *Jenišův Újezd, a part of the matrix of factor scores.*

Factor scores of principal components

1	grave 1	−3.	1.560	0.042	−1.702	−0.248	−0.277
2	grave 2	1.	1.529	−0.142	−1.257	−0.095	−0.152
3	grave 3	−3.	−0.624	−0.516	−1.047	−0.084	−0.113
4	grave 4	1.	2.109	−0.108	0.368	−1.261	−0.270
5	grave 5	1.	3.082	−0.004	0.201	−0.927	0.441
6	grave 6	−5.	−0.556	−0.868	0.259	−0.763	−1.181
7	grave 7	−4.	−0.319	−0.947	0.615	−1.295	−0.555
8	grave 8	2.	−0.273	3.761	1.252	−0.451	0.617
9	grave 9	−3.	−0.612	−0.652	−1.019	0.628	−0.419
10	grave 10	−4.	−0.479	−0.662	0.605	−0.836	−0.292
11	grave 11	5.	0.558	0.362	−0.644	2.447	3.701
12	grave 12	3.	1.596	−0.534	2.535	−0.401	−0.556
13	grave 13	2.	−0.378	3.380	0.485	−1.024	−0.001
14	grave 14	1.	2.030	−0.965	−0.139	−0.323	−1.355

which scored high in relation to this factor (111 out of the 175 bronze artifacts found in 120 analysed graves). Typical are graves with bracelets, anklets and bronze fibulae, which are mostly found at the neck or at the breast of the skeletons. Girdles are common. There are no weapons; armlets, lignite, iron fibulae (and iron in general), remnants of textile, remnants of coffins and fibulae on the shoulder are not diagnostic. Measurements taken on the graves are slightly above the average for all graves.

Factor 2:   Almost all the graves with weapons score high on this factor (spearheads, swords, shields). The high loading on iron artifacts is clearly related to the abundance of weapons. Otherwise only girdles and remnants of textiles are comparatively frequent. There is only one ring ornament, and fibulae of all kinds and positions are not diagnostic. All the measurements taken on the graves are considerably higher than the average.

Factor +3:   All the graves with factor scores equal to or greater than 1 contained one or more iron fibulae, typically at the shoulder. With the exception of left-hand bracelets few other items, though present in small quantities, seem to be diagnostic. The measurements of the graves tend to be average.

Factor −3: A great many graves had a factor score equal to or less than −1. This fact requires further study, as it is not obvious at the first glance which items of the grave furniture could be made responsible for this phenomenon. None of the graves contained an iron fibula or any sort of fibula at the shoulder. In general, the equipment of these graves was rather poor. The measurements of the graves approximate the average.

Factor +4: Armlets, mostly of lignite, both on the right and the left arms, are typically found together with remnants of coffins and possibly fibulae at the shoulders. Measurements of the graves are slightly above the average.

Factor −4: A small number of graves with problems similar to those of Factor −3.

Factor +5: Possibly diagnostic of this factor are graves with a small quantity of ring ornaments. The only typical artifact, however, is bracelet type −4/4 (Waldhauser 1978, table 20) which is known to be found in child graves. There are no anklets and no weapons. The measurements taken on the graves are significantly smaller than the average.

Factor −5: With the exception of the measures, which show very high values, there seems to be nothing especially diagnostic about this grave group.

Vector synthesis does nothing more than what has been described so far. The factors obtained are formal constructs which can be interpreted by means of the methods described in chapter 6.

5.3.5 Structures in non-linear space

Many, if not most archaeological spaces, are not linear. The non-linearity is usually caused either by the inclusion of nominal variables or by missing values. Although a small number of missing values can be substituted by various means, it is dangerous to replace too many of them: any such substitution neglects the individuality and possible specificity of an archaeological object. As to the inclusion of 'false zeros' resulting from the use of nominal variables, a small number of them in the starting matrix may not inflict much harm upon the results, but it is certainly not a logically sound procedure to include any of them. However, when some kind of real numbers are substituted for the missing values in a non-linear archaeological space, the methods of vector synthesis would still work and the results might be quite sensible, especially if the structures contained in the finds are strong. It is unpredictable when such a 'synthesis' will collapse because the vectors will reflect the substituted values and the 'false zeros' more than the logically sound elements of the space. Thus, the use of the methods developed for the linear case must be avoided if the starting space is not linear.

The mathematical procedures applied for the synthesis of structures in a non-linear space are, of course, less satisfactory than vector synthesis. They either use only a small part of the information contained in the descriptive system, or they impose a very special kind of structure on the archaeological record. Therefore, they should not be exploited unnecessarily (i.e. in cases where the data are perfectly suitable for some kind of vector synthesis) just because their mathematical algorithms are more simple to understand or because they are well known from earlier archaeological publications.

Most of the methods aiming at the synthesis of structures in a non-linear space belong to the group called *cluster analysis*. Its products are clusters of objects (less frequently of descriptors), which are arranged into groups according to their 'similarity'. Each object belongs to just *one* cluster, while in vector synthesis each object and/or descriptor may belong to several 'factors' at the same time. This is an important difference, as already our daily life experience suggests that 'things', measuring several 'dimensions', may be attributable to more than one 'cluster' of the real world (for example, a brooch can express a period of archaeological time, a way of dressing, social status, etc., all at the same time).

The final result of most of the varieties of 'cluster analysis' is a graph (in the sense of the mathematical theory of graphs) consisting of 'vertices' (usually archaeological objects) and 'edges', i.e. lines joining the vertices. A typical example of such a graph is the dendrogram well known from many archaeological applications. The use of cluster analysis ending in dendrograms has been taken over from biology where it is believed to reflect the splitting of evolutionary trees. This may have some sense in biology, if evolution is the main dimension of change. However, when used for the classification of stone axes in archaeology, there is hardly any excuse for *imposing* the form of a dendrogram upon the archaeological facts: using the hierarchical cluster analysis ending in a dendrogram, we preselect a particular form of structure into which the facts are then squeezed. This logical flaw does not prevent individual archaeological dendrograms from discovering important structures in archaeological contexts: I have already stressed the fact that on the condition of strong structuring ties in a context almost any algorithm does well. The popularity of dendrograms in archaeology may not result exclusively from the easy availability of computer programs for this peculiar method but also from the fact that their output is graphical, thus pleasing the archaeological affection for figures.

The inadequacy of dendrograms can be made somewhat less acute by using the *minimum spanning tree* (Neustupný 1973b) as the model for the solution (this method has a predecessor, less rigorous from the mathematical point of view, in the so-called close proximity analysis – cf. Renfrew and Sterud 1969). The algorithm for the construction of the spanning tree does not suppose any particular structure in advance, but the identification of clusters is more subjective than with dendrograms. To show how a method from this group works, I shall describe it in more detail in the following paragraphs.

The method starts with identifying a set of archaeological objects with vertices of a mathematical graph. Some measures of similarity, correlation, distance, etc. between the objects is computed (this step does not necessarily imply linearity as many similarity coefficients can be computed even for nominal data). Thus, each object (vertex) is connected to each other by a tie (edge), whose measure is the similarity coefficient. Now, by means of a rather simple algorithm a graph can be constructed such that:

(1) it contains all the vertices (archaeological objects);
(2) it contains no circles (i.e. the graph does not include any sequence of edges that connect any vertex with itself; the graph may branch, but it must never 'return');
(3) the edges used for the construction of the graph are selected in such a way that their sum be maximum (for similarities or correlations) or minimum (for distances).

The graph fulfilling the first two conditions is called a *tree*, while that fulfilling all three conditions is a minimum (or maximum) spanning tree. Any tree containing n vertices has the maximum of $n-1$ edges, which means that less than n coefficients of the original matrix are used. However, it is usually only the edges connected with the highest similarities that enter the tree. For example, if a matrix of correlations is used, the negative correlations do not influence the results at all (although some of them are highly significant from the statistical point of view). This fact is, of course, of advantage if a matrix of nominal variables is used: in such a case the correlations calculated from 'false' zeros are always negative and, as a result, do not influence the final configuration of the graph. This is one of the reasons why this method accepts non-linear archaeological spaces.

The minimum (or maximum) spanning tree is frequently not unique, but parallel solutions are almost always very close to each other. The groups of objects that lie close together on the graph can be proved to be archaeologically meaningful; it is, however, not easy to delimit such groups (or clusters) objectively (e.g. Bujna 1982).

Clustering methods based on the graphical background are not the only choice; by means of computers, clusters can be built using other non-graphical procedures (e.g. the stepwise construction of clusters). It is to be expected that still other methods for the generation of structures in a non-linear space will be devised in the future.

5.3.6 *The confirmatory approach*

No archaeological structures need be presupposed before the exploratory variety of the archaeological synthesis starts; performing the confirmatory variety, however, some knowledge of the structures is indispensable.

The well-known statistical tests are in fact elementary confirmatory procedures. To test, for example, whether male and female graves of a particular culture group differ in the presence of girdle clasps, one has to assume that male and female graves are archaeological structures described by means of descriptors such as girdle clasps. Subsequently, it is possible to test similarly other items of the grave equipment developing something analogical to 'factors' of the exploratory case. This can be done by means of the χ^2 test, correlation coefficients, or a number of other means; it is also possible to use methods from the 'analysis of variance' family. More complicated confirmatory procedures include discrimination analysis, often used in archaeology.

I shall not discuss these statistical tools in more detail as they are well known to many archaeologists and quite frequently used by them. They are discussed at length in many handbooks (e.g. Sokal and Rohlf 1981), some of them compiled especially for archaeologists (e.g. Doran and Hodson 1975; Shennan 1988). The most powerful ones among these methods are based on a number of assumptions about the statistical distribution of the 'variables'; there is a lot of statistics, however, which is 'non-parametric', i.e. free of any such assumptions.

In the early days of the recognition of the role of mathematics in archaeology, the contribution of 'simple' statistics was considerable. The easy availability of computer software combined with the general access to computers in many parts of the world led to a general preference for the use of more complicated multivariate methods, which were often difficult to understand for beginners, and quite often unnecessary. I do not see how anybody can use the discrimination analysis effectively without deep prior experience with testing of statistical distributions, etc. The present-day unsatisfactory situation may improve in the future: the role of confirmatory methods in developed natural sciences makes it clear that archaeological interest in them will revive.

6

Interpretation

In the course of the many transformations described in chapter 3, past live cultures have changed into the archaeological record, which is static, formal, object orientated and mute. Human culture has been transformed into dead things, drastically reduced not only from the point of view of their quantity but also of their quality. Many wooden houses, for example, have disappeared altogether, and most of those that have left any traces do not appear as houses during archaeological excavations, but as incomplete patterns of postholes (i.e. as another entity).

In spite of the fact that archaeological analysis necessarily uses models derived from some kind of living reality, mainly in order to select the appropriate descriptive systems, the subsequent generation of archaeological structures is a formal procedure. As a result, archaeological structures, produced by synthesis, are formal regularities contained in the *record*; they are in no way laws of past human *societies*. The language used by specialists during the treatment of *archaeological means* reflects this formalism: archaeologists, when speaking about their records, often do not express themselves in terms relating to something that we know from everyday life. Concepts such as (archaeological) type, culture group or (chronological) phase make it sufficiently obvious.

In the past, this was one of the main reasons for misunderstandings on the part of historians and cultural anthropologists, whose language was always nearer to 'life' than that spoken by archaeologists. The historians either assumed that the formal archaeological terms could be *translated* into their terms by a very simple procedure (the density of finds, for example, could be 'interpreted' as the density of a population), or they assumed that archaeological knowledge was incompatible with theirs because of the incompatible vocabulary. Many archaeologists also accepted these views.

Archaeological interpretation, as understood in this book, is the procedure within archaeological methodology that *interprets structures* in terms of dynamic concepts compatible with our modern thought. This interpretation is no simple translation, because the 'language' of the archaeological record and the language of history differ in principle. While the language of the archaeological record by itself is incapable of expressing any sort of dynamics or, more generally, any idea which includes the concept of time, the language of history is unthinkable without time-coordinates, explicit or implict. Archaeological interpretation clearly has two functions: first, it returns dead things to life and, second, it retells the story of these things in a language comprehensible to modern mankind. These two functions of interpretation, however, are two inseparable aspects of a single intellectual procedure.

What is described as interpretation in this book is often termed explanation in other circumstances. I see no reason why the two terms could not be used for the same notion interchangeably; it has to be remembered, however, that 'explanation' has an established meaning in the so-called philosophy of science.

For me, archaeological interpretation is historical interpretation, i.e. expression of the regularities of the record in terms of the concepts of history. In this connection, I would like to explain shortly what I understand as 'history'. Any human society, past or present, consists of both 'synchronic' and 'diachronic' relations among individuals and among groups of individuals. In archaeology, the synchronic relations pertain to the function, meaning and significance of archaeological structures; they relate to the logics according to which a society 'works' at a certain moment (or period) of time. From the synchronic point of view, archaeology can be joined with anthropology (cf. Binford 1962).

At the same time, however, archaeology includes the diachronic aspect, i.e. relations that change through time. These are the same relations as in the synchronic case, so it would be unwise to separate them by a hard and fast line.

Archaeological structures change in time in a most varied and complex way. Some of the changes have been described as evolution and others as diffusion; these are certainly not the only forms of change that constitute history. Yet, diachronic studies are often placed into 'history' and considered as an almost absolute contradiction to 'anthropology'. As I see it, both synchronic and diachronic aspects of the human past can be conveniently housed under the concept of history. This can be understood as a social science in spite of its close contacts with many natural scientific disciplines. The fact that a natural science studies archaeological ecofacts does not turn it into a social science.

If archaeology is to become a historical discipline in the sense outlined above, it should demonstrate that:

(1)   the regularities contained in archaeological structures are *reflections of the laws regulating past human societies* and, at the same time, *reflections of their history;*

(2)   it is possible, on the basis of archaeological structures and on the basis of laws observable in living societies, to restore the essential knowledge about the past.

It does not seem to be very difficult to prove the first thesis. If any non-natural regularities or patterns are recognized in the archaeological record by means of synthesis, they can be assumed to have originated by two processes only: either as a reflection of the structuring of the human past, or as a reflection of later transformations which the records passed following their 'exit' (cf. Urbańczyk 1986). Theoretically, it should be sufficient to separate the effect of the possible transformations to get the required result. This need not be a simple task in specific research situations. Let us recall the well-known problem whether observed fluctuations in the number of sites known from different periods of prehistory in many parts of the world reflect fluctuations in the density of past populations or whether they simply indicate different patterns of the destructive and quantitative transformations of the archaeological record.

The second thesis is much more difficult to prove; materialist philosophies, however, make it easier to accept. If similar material conditions of life produce similar social structures and these, in turn, generate corresponding superstructures, than it is possible, on the basis of a model formed outside an archaeological context, to make judgements on many aspects of past life. It is often believed that such judgements are to start from the so-called productive forces (i.e. more or less 'economy') and be directed towards the so-called super-structure or the 'spiritual life'. In many practical applications it is exactly the opposite procedure which is followed: archae-ologists start from superstructure phenomena, such as grave rituals, to elucidate problems of material production. The rest of this chapter is more or less concerned with questions associated with the second thesis.

It should be stressed at this point that this problem is not necessarily connected with the incompleteness of the archaeo-logical record such as is caused by the disintegration of organic substances. The fact, however, that present-day archae-ologists are denied access to those aspects of past life which are tied exclusively or predominantly to language (such as songs, tales, etc.) is disquieting. It is undeniable that our archaeology is seriously incomplete in this respect and, at the time when this book is being written, there are no non-science-fiction perspectives for the solution of the problem.

6.1   Categories of the live culture

People think in notions (or concepts) and the words of our languages are denotations for these concepts. The fact that texts written in all the known 'modern' languages all over the world can be mutually translated (notwithstanding some difficulties), proves that the concepts of modern mankind are more or less universal. There are reasons to believe that this situation has been in existence at least since the beginnings of the late palaeolithic period. This is the basis for the belief that our own experience with concepts can be transferred back in time.

We have seen in chapter 5 how the archaeological record, the 'dead' culture, can be conceptualized in terms of *archaeo-logical*, i.e. material, *structures*. Living culture, which can be particularized into facts ('living' facts), is structured somewhat differently; its structuring units are described here as *categories* (of the living culture), a construct similar to what is usually termed a notion or a concept. In addition to function, meaning and significance, the categories of the living culture also have their material structure. There is no doubt that function, meaning and significance relate to the substance of categories; they can be described as their *contents*. The material structure, up to the transformations identical with the archaeological structure of analogical archaeological facts, is clearly a *form* of this contents. The living categories also have another form, a designation by means of a word of a natural language. While the material structure can be denoted as the internal form of the categories, the denotation is more or less their external, arbitrary form.

It is important to note that individual facts do not define any category; they possess a material structure exclusively in the sense that it is contained in them. Individual facts also have no function, meaning or significance, theirs is only *use*. The function of an axe is apparently not digging holes in the ground, although any individual specimen of an axe can be successfully *used* for this purpose. Individual facts have mostly no proper name; the word employed for them in natural languages is their generic name, i.e. the word which denotes their category.

Let us repeat once more at this point that, in full analogy with dead structures, the function of categories is their 'practical' purpose, i.e. the way they are usually used during human intercourse with nature; meaning is the social environment of categories, while significance is their mental environment. Under most circumstances, categories have some function, some meaning and some significance *at the same time*. The obvious reason for this is the fact that *everything which humans do is done within society, and everything passes through human consciousness*. The function of a house is obviously protection against bad weather; its meaning may be that it brings a family together, consolidating and strengthening its internal ties. If it is also the place where ghosts or souls of ancestors dwell, this is its significance (or, more properly, one of its many possible significances); the house becomes an arbitrary sign.

Most categories of material culture are determined by their function and/or meaning. It would be unsound, however, to maintain that categories have no significance. What is usually called functionalism makes the function absolute. Its contradiction is ethnological structuralism; some recent adherents of this school apparently believe that artifacts (and even some ecofacts) have only symbolic significance, as they do not discuss their practical use. Both functionalists and structuralists largely neglect what is called meaning in this volume.

From the archaeological point of view, however, the principal question relating to the structure of categories is the relation between their material structure on the one hand, and their function, meaning and significance on the other. If this relation were fully arbitrary, the effort to compare prehistoric and living artifacts on the basis of their material structure would be futile. We know from everyday experience that there is indeed a close correspondence between the material structure of categories of facts and their function and meaning.

For example, a flat iron object with a butt for a wooden handle at the one end and a sharp edge at the opposite end is clearly an axe. Its function in our modern society is chopping wood, (rarely) cutting trees and/or shaping small wooden objects. The meaning of the steel axe is traditional household, as outside it the axe has a rather limited purpose. It has no widespread symbolic significance in western societies. Almost any member of a modern community will recognize the artifact whose material structure was described above, and will be able to connect it with at least a subset of its functions.

When there is no butt, no preserved handle, a rather narrow edge, and the material is not iron (steel) but stone, few people will identify the artifact as an axe unless they know it from a museum, or at least from a photograph in a book on archaeology. A model, in cases like this usually derived from ethnography, is needed to recognize the function of the artifact.

6.2   The concept of an archaeological model

An archaeological model, in its most simple aspect, is a proposition expressing the relation between the contents of a category of the material culture and its form, i.e. the relation between function, meaning and significance on the one side, and the material structure on the other side. 'Storing liquids' is one of the functions of a material structure which can be described by a series of attributes and terms 'amphora'. The proposition 'the function of amphorae is the storing of liquids' is a simple (functional) model. In more complicated cases, models are networks of such propositions.

There arises an important problem whether these relations are unique, i.e. whether they can be conceptualized as a one-to-one correspondence, a particular function (meaning, significance) always implying the same material structure and, vice versa, a particular material structure always implying the same function (meaning, significance). The assumption of such a one-to-one correspondence has in fact been adopted by those archaeologists who use ethnographic parallels (or analogies) for interpreting the findings of archaeology. Namely if a one-to-one relation should hold between a particular form of the material culture on the one side, and a particular function, meaning and/or significance on the other side, it would be obvious that in the case where the material forms of an archaeological and an ethnographical phenomenon coincided, their function (and possibly also their meanings and significances) should also be the same.

There is ample evidence that one and the same *function* can be served by a set of very different material structures. Drinking can be realized by means of a cup (handled or unhandled), a beaker, a mug or even a bowl. Bark, wood, fired clay and metal would all be suitable for such drinking vessels. The variability of material things able to carry one and the same *meaning* is, of course, immense and there are hardly any limits to the material structures able to express one particular *significance*. Extraordinarily rich persons may be interred outside communal cemeteries, but the poorest ones may be treated in the same way. There are innumerable symbols to express the concept of fertility.

Very similar or even identical material structures may have more than one function, meaning and, of course, significance. A 'house' as a pattern of postholes, for example, would originally have had the function of sheltering people, but in certain instances of the neolithic period in Europe there are grounds to believe that some of the 'houses' in fact served as graves. Graves of females equipped with unusually rich personal ornaments may indicate that the leading social class included women, but it can also convey the information that husbands (or owners) of those females were rich (the females themselves could have been serfs). It is difficult to decide whether all the varieties of small sun symbols of the eneolithic period in Central Europe had the same significance, if they appear exclusively in male graves in the Globular Amphora culture and exclusively in graves of women in the developed phases of the Corded Ware cultures.

Although there is no one-to-one correspondence between function (or meaning, or significance) and the material structure of categories, *the number of highly probable possibilities is still very limited*, especially as function is concerned. Thus, there is a limited number of probable models. This fact often makes modelling a matter of choice, but it in no case allows archaeologists to form models (or hypotheses, if another idiom is used) on the basis of completely free will or 'hallucination'.

Let us assume that what is needed is the explanation of a prehistoric cemetery. The creation of a model of such a cemetery depends on a number of other models, for example on an assumption of how various sex and age classes of prehistoric communities can be reflected in the 'material' culture. In this case, several models are joined into a network in which the individual constituents are connected in a logical manner. To put it in other words, complex models have the *form* of theories, which may be less apparent in the case of individual statements. In the hands of archaeologists, however, they do not become theories until they are successfully tested against archaeological structures.

If a number of simple models are connected into a model of higher order by means of logical and causal links, the probability of the whole network usually increases, especially if the constituent models are mutually independent. Thus, *the categories of living cultures become building stones of archaeological models*: their connection and inclusion into models, however, is not random: they must obey the logics of the real world which is studied by all the social sciences. At the same time, they must take account of the historical conditions of the particular time and place for which the model is being constructed. The conception of categories as building stones or elements of large-scale systems (models) enables archaeologists to generate models which are logical and historical at the same time: they can be accommodated to the concreteness of the archaeological sources. A model, taken as a whole, need not reproduce any 'observable' situation (e.g. an ethnographic parallel).

If models were transmitted to archaeology from some living culture as *wholes*, it would never be possible to form a model for a past situation which did not repeat itself later. Archaeologists would be limited to situations reappearing in some (still) living society. Such limitations were in fact accepted by those who tried to interpret archaeological findings on the basis of so-called *ethnographic parallels* (*analogies*): they could never get behind the observations of the ethnographers. Let us note that simple analogies were also derived from some historical parallels, or even from our contemporary life; they have exactly the same status as the parallels with ethnographic observations.

As we have already noted earlier, ethnographic analogies assume a one-to-one correspondence between the form and the contents of categories of the material culture; it follows from the preceding paragraphs that they do not allow for the historical concreteness of archaeological situations. It is for these reasons that they form an unsuitable basis for explanation in archaeology. Yet, in the history of our discipline, ethnographic analogies played an important role. It is often believed that they were discarded mainly because of the untenable principles behind them and, at the same time, because of their unsuccessful applications. It should be kept in mind, however, that the criticism of ethnographic analogies came more or less with the advent of the typological paradigm, in the framework of which the space left for explanations remained rather narrow in general. It should be made clear that the critical attitude towards *ethnographic analogies* in no way implies a refusal of any *role of ethnography* in the archaeological method.

General models, advocated in this book, try to select from particular cases only the substantial relations between material structures and their function, meaning and significance. It is in this way that they fight the non-historicity, which is so typical of ethnographic analogies. Let us consider society in the Central European eneolithic period. To its model we shall not look for an ethnographic group that lived in the conditions of early developing metallurgy, because any such group lived under some kind of historical conditions which were necessarily different from those assumed for the archaeological case. Rules governing the modelled society will be deduced from the study of several groups supposed to reflect that particular social environment, stripped of the historical peculiarities. General models lack the concreteness of ethnographic analogies. However, because they are constructed of categories (which are their 'building stones'), they can be used to match almost any kind of archaeological structures. The case of the lower palaeolithic, where some of the 'building stones' are missing, will be discussed later.

Each model has not only its qualitative aspect (the individual material structures and their contents) but also its *quantitative side*. It is not sufficient to establish that prehistoric ploughing was impossible without a certain degree of stabilization of herds; it is also necessary to find out what consequences this stabilization had for the quantitative composition of the herd, for the pattern of killings and for the reproduction of the animals. For example, it can be assumed that each family should sustain at least a pair of draft animals over the winter to make it possible to till fields in the spring; this requirement presupposes a certain number of animals to enable their reproduction, etc. Any well-developed model should be both qualitative and quantitative.

6.3 The generation of archaeological models

In general, archaeological models are derived from the knowledge of human societies which can be studied in their dynamic form, i.e. in running time. In the case of models stemming from ethnography or ethnoarchaeology this principle is obviously fulfilled. It has already been argued that the words of which historical (written) sources consist are able to express dynamics so that they are *in principle* equivalent to

direct observations of living societies. Incidentally, ethnographic reports also reach most archaeologists in the written
form, and are therefore of the same kind as historical records.
It is only in ethnoarchaeological research that at least some
archaeologists make actual observations; and even then the
results are mediated by means of the language of the
observers to most of their colleagues.

However, any results of observation of a contemporary or
historical society can become a source of archaeological
models; sociology, economy and demography are well-
known examples. Our own everyday life is another source of
models; it is difficult for any archaeologist to dispose of, or not
to be influenced by, this 'most natural' frame of reference
which suggests itself as self-evident. One of the most
promising fields of contemporary life used for the generation
of models in our discipline is undoubtedly what is known as
experimental archaeology; contemporary everyday life lived
by means of 'archaeological' artifacts.

It is common practice, although a rather dangerous one, to
derive models for an archaeological context from another
archaeological context assumed to be already 'interpreted'.
Using such 'internal' archaeological models is *the usual manner
in which developed paradigms work*: as these models are not
apparent at first sight, archaeology seems to be self-sufficient
with *no models* at all.

The statements on the sources of archaeological models
presented in the foregoing paragraphs are not universally
accepted. Some archaeologists believe that models (which
they call hypotheses) can be taken from any source, even from
hallucination. The source of a model is assumed to be irrele-
vant, the only important fact is how hypotheses stand up
when tested against archaeological facts (cf. Binford 1968). It
seems to me that this view is connected with the survival of
the idea that a scientist, while approaching his object, does not
know anything about it. However, as argued earlier, this does
not appear to be a realistic attitude: there is always a preliminary interpretation determined by the previous development
of archaeology. Thus, when finding a particular artifact during
excavation of a site, archaeologists assume that they have
found a pot or a weapon or another specifiable artifact. It

would be absurd to demand that this knowledge should be erased and replaced by a hypothesis based on hallucination.

The question of the generation of models is also a problem of the effectiveness of the archaeological method. The testing of very many hypotheses (all of them more or less equivalent starting points) could take a very long time indeed before the right one would be encountered. The following paragraphs explain an alternative way to the problem.

The most simple procedure for the generation of a model of an archaeological context would be, of course, to take over a description of an ethnographical or historical society, including its material culture. This would create a *parallel* whose constituent parts might not be connected logically; in most cases, they are just described as observed. The risk of using such a parallel would be, for example, a form of architecture in an ethnographical community might depend on some kind of specific climate more than on social organization, or that the forms of some artifacts might be determined by a specific cultural tradition more than by their function. What an archaeologist needs is clearly not a parallel whose elements depend on conditions of place and time different from his context, but a model whose elements are mutually connected by means of logical and causal relations. The principal question is how such a model can be built.

It is clearly advantageous to assume as little as possible at the beginning: to select a *key category* (including its material structure), and to develop it further logically, using the knowledge both of the laws regulating living societies and of the 'historical' circumstances of the context to be modelled (i.e. its conditioning by place and time). The key category, however, has to be chosen in such a way that it should be an element of the archaeological context and, at the same time, should express its substantial aspect. The key category (or a small group of categories) will therefore be very *abstract* (i.e. poor in properties); it is only during its building up that it becomes more *concrete*, i.e. rich in details. A model constructed in this way would be both strictly *logical* (being developed deductively) and *historical* because its generation would be conditioned by the limits of time and space suggested by the archaeological context.

I shall explain this methodology briefly by means of the example of eneolithic society in Central Europe. The key category of the model becomes the *wooden ard*, attested for this period indirectly by means of a number of very strong arguments such as plough furrows and the widespread exploitation of cattle for traction. The ard is a very abstract notion indeed (it is very simple even as an archaeological 'type'), but it seems to contain *in itself* the system on which eneolithic society worked. The further logical development of the model is as follows. The use of the ard presupposes a highly developed form of cattle breeding (a historical condition!) as it is unthinkable without regular reproduction of the cattle in a stabilized herd of domestic animals with at least partial winter feeding. This is one aspect of the model. The other is the fact that the wooden ard fosters more or less permanent fields (to exclude the regeneration of roots) and thus ends the period of exclusive slash-and-burn agriculture. The stability of fields means greater stability of prehistoric settlement in general.

At the same time, the ard implies a deep change in the natural division of labour, i.e. the division of economic activities as performed by men and women, adults and children. While both genders play an approximately equal role in agriculture based on the slash-and-burn method (the role of men being usually the keeping of domestic animals and/or hunting while the main sphere of women is in the care for fields), the tillage of fields by means of an ard is an exclusive opportunity for men. In this way, men 'seized' the majority of activities pertaining to the acquisition of food, while women were ousted to subsidiary activities in the production of staples and to services for the family. These relations created a number of specific social relations which are summed up in the concept of 'patriarchy' (the model is not being developed here in any detail).

It is obvious that the model generated in this way has the form of a theory. At the same time, it is testable by means of archaeological structures in many points: it presupposes the ard, a specific type of animal breeding, more or less permanent fields and stable settlement sites, a clearly developed opposition of the genders, certain preference of men within the society etc.

Let us note how few pieces of ethnographic knowledge have been used in this model; also, that they are of a rather general nature. When the model is 'tested' by means of the archaeological evidence coming from a lot of cultural groups in Central Europe (such as the Globular Amphora and the Corded Ware cultures), it becomes a theory which is not contained in any ethnographical or historical 'parallel' of which I am aware: neither ethnography nor history describes any 'patriarchal' society whose economy is based on the breeding of cattle and the growing of cereals on non-irrigated fields: this seems to be a historical peculiarity of a limited area of the Old World which was so much progressive that it was replaced by more developed social systems everywhere before the advent of writing. In consequence of this no 'parallel' can explain the eneolithic period in Central Europe and some neighbouring regions.

Those readers who are acquainted with nineteenth-century German philosophy may have noticed the similarity of the algorithm proposed in the foregoing paragraphs with Hegel's *ascent from the abstract to the concrete*, a part of his dialectical logics. This is, of course, not by chance. There is also a similarity, this time a somewhat more distant one, with the generation of deductive theories in modern formal logics.

When using any of the above named sources of models to extract the 'building stones' of new archaeological models, there arises an important problem: ethnography, for example, almost never formulates general rules, valid in the societies it describes, in such a way that they could be directly used by archaeologists. This is caused partly by the fact that many ethnographical reports were written during the reign of old paradigms in ethnography, partly by the fact that 'modern' ethnography, having its own problems, quite often pays little attention to what has been described in the preceding paragraphs as the categories of the material culture. The formulation of many 'rules' is therefore left to archaeologists, who are then inclined to use 'the best fitting' parallel instead of a model. Moreover, archaeologists looking for the general rules working among existing societies are often in the position of laymen, with all the complications implied. No university training in 'anthropology' can remove this flaw.

Some of the above mentioned sources of models, such as economics or sociology, do formulate rules or laws directly but, in spite of the fact that generality or even universality is assumed, they mostly relate to modern societies of the western type. This can be another source of misunderstanding, as any particular context met by archaeologists is historical. To correlate, for example, sociology with material culture is no simple task.

Since 1970 there have appeared two new sources of archaeological models which are expected to be especially productive in the future. A short separate treatment of these two sources in the following paragraphs does not suggest, however, that they should replace completely all the other sources of models used traditionally.

6.3.1   *The role of ethnoarchaeology*

Ethnoarchaeology has grown from the need of archaeologists to look at the surviving societies from the point of view of archaeology, i.e. it tries to study the possible correlation between the material culture of peoples on the one side and the 'unobservable' social relations and/or spiritual life on the other side. An explanation of the material phenomena of the culture studied is achieved in this way, and it is believed to bear on the explanation of similar archaeological phenomena appearing in other cultures. If the transfer of the explanation from the ethnoarchaeological case to the purely archaeological one is conceived as an 'ethnographical parallel', this is just another case of the method already criticized. Quite often, however, ethnoarchaeological research is simply meant to find out the various ways in which 'material culture' can reflect (or express) the 'non-material' aspects of culture.

Ethnoarchaeology of simple non-European societies is clearly *superior* to ethnography in that it systematically takes into account the material culture; this is especially valid if the observations are worked up by means of archaeological methods, including the extraction of archaeological structures. The fact that ethnoarchaeological observations make it easy (at least in theory) to quantify, is another advantage: it is rare that the data of 'pure' ethnography contain information on measures, counts, frequencies, etc. Ethnoarchaeology, however, has two considerable *disadvantages*: first, it becomes more and more difficult to perform in a world where simple non-industrial societies are quickly disappearing and, second, its success is strongly conditioned by the selection of questions which the ethnoarchaeologists ask; in this respect, it resembles usual ethnography.

Archaeologists working as ethnoarchaeologists can follow the formal differentiation of culture and seek its cognitive explanation; they can plot the spatial distribution of various cultural phenomena and correlate them, for example with partitions within the live society. They cannot compare the observed time changes of the culture observed by them with the time changes known from prehistory, as the time scales differ substantially: the ethnoarchaeologically observed changes operate within the span of a few years while the archaeological changes are matters of decades and centuries. The cognitive explanation, as supplied by the peoples who use the culture studied by the ethnoarchaeologists, is often a *subjective reflection* of some deep and hidden social principles not realized by the peoples themselves. This is, of course, something which good ethnoarchaeological research should take into account.

The scope of ethnoarchaeology can be widened if its methods are applied not only to the traditional 'simple' cultures such as that of the Eskimos or the Australian aborigines, but to all possible human cultures. This approach has already been applied in the case of the archaeology of rubbish (cf. Megaw 1984). Any other sphere of modern life can be studied similarly, and the still remembered experience of recently extinct technologies or social institutions can be exploited. While using such sources of models to be applied for the interpretation of prehistoric contexts, it is always necessary to consider carefully all the historical conditions influencing modern or sub-modern cultures; this, of course, should be done with any source of any archaeological model.

There is a cultural continuity in many parts of the world reaching from prehistoric up to the sub-modern times and virtually no change can be imagined to have stepped in. One of the examples is the milking of cows. I showed a set of earthenware prehistoric vessels to several old women in southern Bohemia who still milked their cows manually some thirty years ago, asking them to select the 'types' inappropriate for milking. They pointed to some of the prehistoric forms, and they all agreed on something that might be surprising to an academic archaeologist: pottery in general is unsuitable for the purpose because many cows kick during milking. A ceramic vessel would crack, while a wooden or metal receptacle would withstand the damage. From this elementary ethnoarchaeological research it becomes obvious that it is necessary either to assume familiarity with wooden vessels for the purpose of milking in prehistory, or to assume that the difficulty with kicking was solved in another way.

6.3.2   The role of experimental archaeology

Experimental archaeology has developed as a 'discipline' over the last few decades and, in a remarkable number of cases, it is performed by non-archaeologists, whose interest is only partly 'scientific'. Many practitioners of archaeological experiments believed that they had proved some archaeological thesis, such as that stone 'battle-axes' served as tools because they were shown, by means of experiments, to be apt for this purpose. The persuasion of the experimenters in this respect was corroborated by the fact that many of them used actual prehistoric tools taken from archaeological collections. This view, of course, has aroused much controversy as there is clearly a difference between what *could* happen and what *did* happen. If experimental archaeology would really be in a position to prove any part of archaeological theory, most other parts of the discipline would become superfluous or would be reduced to the role of 'helpers' for the experimentors. This thesis is hardly acceptable to most archaeologists.

Archaeological experiments form a poor analogy to experiments in the natural sciences. In the latter case everything, including the 'force' that starts the experiment and keeps it running, is natural. With archaeological experiments the active factor of the experiment, the human factor, is not genuine (ancient) but modern; it is impossible to involve in the experiment genuine prehistoric people with their exact knowledge of ancient technology, ancient resources, social and mental conditions for their action, etc. However exact copies of archaeological artifacts the experiment uses, the experimenter himself is a *model* of a prehistoric or historical person and, therefore, the result of the experiment itself cannot represent more than a model. It is just in their role of *sources of models* that 'experiments' in archaeology may gain in power in the future.

Most archaeologists know what difference there is between taking a photograph of a prehistoric pot and making a drawing of it, however ugly the drawing may be. After taking the photograph, the archaeologist knows in fact very little about his vessel, while by drawing it he or she cannot escape noting various relations (e.g. between the diameter of the rim and the diameter of the base), the irregularities of walls, the exact position of handles etc. This is because the drawing is an elementary (two-dimensional) reproduction of the vessel. The archaeologist would learn even more about it by using colours. But he could claim an exact knowledge of his artifact only if he were able to reproduce it exactly as an undistinguishable copy in three dimensions.

Some of the producers of archaeological fakes are able to do the job, but most archaeologists, among them specialists on prehistoric pottery, would be unable to make a pot even approximately, and many specialists in other fields of prehistoric 'crafts' would get into a similarly precarious position when asked to manifest their abilities to reproduce 'their' artifacts. It is certainly not the task of archaeology to imitate archaeological finds, but it is at least interesting to note that during the reign of the typological paradigm almost no archaeologist was able to produce things similar to prehistoric artifacts; people who had the knowledge and skill lived on the outskirts of the archaeological community and were mostly considered to be somewhat eccentric.

It is a barbaric habit to experiment directly with archaeological finds, as any modern use of genuine artifacts obliterates the original traces of work and creates new ones which possibly do not correspond to any ancient use. For the purpose of experimenting, replicas are usually as good as the best-preserved originals. Working with them one tries to *rediscover the material algorithms* according to which artifacts and ecofacts were used, and the algorithms according to which artifacts were produced. It ensues that experiments try to find the original function of archaeological facts. The question of recovering meaning and/or significance by means of experiments will be discussed later.

As has already been noted, experiments cannot solve problems: what they can do is to suggest possibilities or *sets of models* to be tested against the archaeological evidence. In some instances it may take a long time before an acceptable solution is discovered, but sometimes efficient algorithms are found quickly (for example the cutting of trees by means of stone axes, ploughing by means of 'iron age' ploughs, etc.).

It happens frequently that archaeologists discover important details during their experimental work; such details are difficult to find on the basis of theoretical models only. During the grinding of prehistoric kinds of wheat, for example, there is a surprising quantity of inedible remains, which could be fed to domestic animals. This would partly supply their need for protein. Experiments have also shown that straw from fields (after the ears have been cut off) can be quite easily cropped by simply pulling handfuls of it out together with the roots and the green undergrowth. In spite of its bad nutritional value it could have been an easily accessible source of winter feed for some of the prehistoric domestic animals, especially in the case of emergency (L. Peške, pers. comm.). It is often believed that straw was not an accessible resource for European farmers before the introduction of the scythe.

The main advantage of archaeological experiments, however, is in the fact that they are performed with *exactly the same 'archaeological structures'* (e.g. the same types of tools) as the corresponding activities of the past. This cannot be achieved while observing any living society. Moreover, many *conditions* in which the experiments operate can be *controlled*. When cutting trees by means of neolithic axes common in Central Europe, it is possible to select those species that really grew there at that time. Also, some aspects of archaeological experiments can be easily *quantified*. As already noted, the main disadvantage is in the fact that the personal agent of the experiments (the archaeologist) is so much different from that of the past. As a whole, archaeological experiments seem to be an important future source of archaeological models, especially as far as the function of ancient artifacts is concerned.

There is no reason to believe that meaning and even significance could not be arrived at by means of experiment; but to achieve something in this field would require a considerably deeper and longer-lasting effort of whole experimental communities. Let us assume for a moment that several groups of our contemporaries set out on a complex experiment of living in the European neolithic style permanently, and neither they nor their descendants want to return into our modern times. It is very likely that the material conditions of their life would create, after some time, the corresponding 'neolithic' social structure and a 'neolithic' ideology. There is no basis to judge how much time this would take.

If the experimenters lived in complete isolation from our modern world (e.g. by not accepting 'immigrants' from the twentieth century), ethnoarchaeologists would find true neolithic communities while visiting them in the future. They would be, no doubt, very near to the European neolithic, but their culture and society could not escape an internal development of both its material and spiritual culture; as a result, there would be hardly any identity with the original model. By the way, these 'neolithic' communities would live according to an obsolete model of the neolithic period, as our present-day knowledge of the period is far from what will be achieved in the twenty-first century. The communities would have to develop this obsolete model into details just in order to survive. Thus, they would become a close parallel but certainly no general model of the European neolithic. The value of such a 'parallel' would be considerable, but in principle it would not differ from the other neolithic parallels already described by ethnography.

It follows from the preceding paragraphs that experimental archaeology is an important source of parallels and models. These models, however, cannot replace the complex archaeological concern with the past.

6.4 The use of models

Archaeologists use models mainly during two stages of their method: analysis and interpretation. There are several points in the course of archaeological synthesis, such as the choice of the appropriate mathematical method, where models are also indispensable. 'Modern' archaeological method is characterized by limiting the number of places where models (or the accumulated previous and parallel knowledge) can enter archaeology. It was typical of the traditional paradigm that what are called models in this chapter were exploited almost any time during the process of generating new knowledge. I believe that this state of affairs will return in a 'more modern' paradigm of the future; at present, however, the clear-cut separation of models into a limited number of phases of the method seems to be justifiable.

6.4.1 Modelling during analysis

The first occasion on which an archaeologist usually meets models is the derivation of the descriptive system of his or her context. Let us assume that the context consists of graves of a cemetery and let us try to derive descriptive systems for two different models, A and B.

> Model A. The context consists of a cemetery where individual graves were added in a time sequence. Presumably it will be possible to ascertain the chronological development of assemblages of artifacts and thus to define chronological phases. Various types of artifacts from the graves, such as pottery, weapons and personal ornaments, will represent other 'archaeological structures' of interest. The meaning of the structures (phases, types) is chronological variability.

In consequence of such a model, the descriptive system for pottery will concentrate on details of shape and decoration patterns, as well as other descriptors known to 'measure' time. The descriptive systems for weapons and personal ornaments will be derived according to similar principles. Facing a concrete context most archaeologists would be able to enumerate lists of descriptors and their states immediately. It is obvious that model A is a typical product of the typological paradigm and, therefore, it limits its inquiry to spatial and temporal variability. The second model, B, tries to go further, overtaking the old paradigm; it does not exhaust, however, all the meaningful questions which can be asked.

> Model B. The context represents a cemetery consisting of grave groups covering groups of persons connected by close social relations (individual families?). The community which the cemetery reflects was a patriarchal type; differentially furnished graves of men and women, adults and children can therefore be expected. It is not excluded that the community was socially differentiated behind groupings based on gender and age. It is to be expected that the cemetery was used over a certain period; not all the graves were contemporary, and there will be some chronological variability. The meaning of structures to be discovered will be the social differentiation within the community, but structures like chronological phases are also to be expected.

In view of the fact that chronological variation may be of importance, one part of the descriptive system will be more or less identical with that of Model A. This system will most probably be applied and synthesized separately. The other part of descriptive system B would consist of classes (not types) of pottery which more probably than types reflect the function of vessels; descriptors such as the volume of vessels, their height, the openness of neck, etc. will be considered important. The classes of weapons and tools will become valuable indicators of the division of labour and activities in general. Personal ornaments may reflect the social status of the deceased. The determination of sex and age by means of the methods of physical anthropology will become indispensable. The position of artifacts and ecofacts within the grave, as well as the dimension of nearly everything, will be demanded. In the case of an actual cemetery the requirements of the model as to the composition of the descriptive system would result in a list of descriptors which, however, need not lead to one single analysis.

It is obvious that, on the whole, Model B leads to a completely different (and more demanding) descriptive system than Model A. It can be expected that completely different structures will result during synthesis based on those systems and, of course, the final interpretation will also differ in the two cases.

6.4.2   *Interpretation by means of modelling*

As soon as the structures of a context are generated, it comes to their interpretation. Here again, models are used. Let us consider Vikletice, a Corded Ware cemetery in Bohemia. It was ascertained on the basis of spatial and chronological analysis of the cemetery that its graves clustered into grave groups in each of which graves of men, women and children were represented in certain stable proportions. Approximately ten graves corresponded to one century within each of the grave groups. A demographic model shows that the same proportions of the sex and age groups as those observed can be expected on the basis of the life tables of the population. The same demographic model leads to the conclusion that one family left approximately ten graves per century (on the condition that children younger than three years did not appear in the cemeteries). All this suggests that the grave groups are to be interpreted as reflections of individual families (Neustupný 1983).

The same cemeteries, however, also contain 'small' grave groups consisting of a few graves each. How to interpret them? According to the demographic model a large proportion of families was unstable: they died out after several years or decades because of the high mortality rate. As a result, if 'large' grave groups (containing tens of graves) are surrounded by many 'small' groups, it fully corresponds to the model of that particular prehistoric society with its demographic instability. Let us note that the model used in these paragraphs must be fairly accurately quantified: an exclusively qualitative consideration of the problem would obviously lead nowhere.

It could be asked whether there is any alternative model that would explain the same structures of the same context (cemetery) equally well or even better. In another model, which did apply in another period of prehistory in the same region, individuals of the same sex were clustered into one group. Clearly, this does not correspond to the structures of Vikletice as derived on the basis of the finds (the two genders are always mixed in the groups in more or less equal proportions). It could also be supposed that the dead were arranged in the cemetery according to their social status, prestige, etc. In this case, the grave goods should differ in the individual grave groups, which is not the case.

The assumption that the arrangement of graves into groups reflects chronological order is difficult to sustain in view of the established chronology of the cemetery. Surprisingly, the idea that the distribution of the dead into the grave groups was entirely random, i.e. without any well-defined conception, is rather difficult to disprove. Within such a model, however, it would not be easy to explain why so many 'complete' grave groups contain ten graves per century. Also, it is well known that events as important as death and interment were rarely regulated by random rules; persons who belonged together during their lives were usually buried next to each other on their death. Undoubtedly, by the exclusion of alternative models the probability of the interpretation gains.

Another simple example of interpretation is the function of stone axes of the European neolithic period. In addition to their shape it is also important to take into consideration the historical conditions under which the tools flourished. Neolithic communities lived (at least in Central Europe) more or less in a forest, be it primary or secondary. Working of wood must therefore have been one of the most frequent activities; apart from the 'axes' or 'adzes', there is no artifact that could fulfil the function. All the ethnographic artifacts of the same shape served for cutting wood. Moreover, some of the ethnographic 'axes' or 'adzes' have the same microscopic traces of work on their cutting edges. The same traces of work have also been produced experimentally. So it is almost certain that the tools in question served as axes or adzes.

From time to time there appears an assumption that neolithic adzes served as plough-shares for wooden ploughs. This alternative model can be safely ruled out. First of all, the Central European neolithic is the period of slash-and-burn agriculture with no ploughing; this is an important historical condition. Then, stone artifacts were almost nowhere used as plough-shares and in the rare cases where they were they did not have the form of neolithic adzes. Finally, when well conserved, neolithic adzes do not show the traces of work obtained on stone adzes used experimentally for ploughing.

6.4.3   The iterative nature of the archaeological method

The task of modelling in the phase of archaeological interpretation is to create theoretical knowledge on the object of archaeology, i.e. on the past understood as a live process. Models of an archaeological context become theory of the context when successfully tested against archaeological structures. This means, however, that the descriptive system, on the basis of which the structures and later their interpretation were derived, has become obsolete: the new theory, if considered as a model, would not allow the creation of a better variant of the descriptive system.

This is a contradiction hidden in every successful application of the archaeological method. The newly obtained theory, which can always be turned into a new model, generates new descriptors and new structures; and the new structures are expected to be given a new explanation. These facts compel the archaeologist to repeat the whole method as soon as he has completed its preceding step. Theoretically the process never ends, because human knowledge is always relative and never absolute. In practical applications, however, the increment of new knowledge becomes negligible after a few steps (iterations), usually because the average level of knowledge in archaeology and in the 'surrounding' disciplines does not allow us to get much further. This means that the whole iterative process stops for some time before new developments in some branch of archaeology allow it to go on.

How the iterative process works in a particular case will be shown by the example of stone axes (which is not based on any real archaeological material).

(1) The first descriptive system may have been derived from some rather general considerations based on an ethnographical parallel; it contained the length, the width, the thickness and presence of the edge. This was processed in the usual way

described in the preceding chapters, and the structure obtained was subsequently interpreted as tools for cutting wood.

(2) Such tools, however, can be classed either as axes or as adzes. (This statement is clearly based on some non-archaeological knowledge.) The difference between them is in their hafting: the edge of an axe is parallel to the long axis of the handle while with an adze the edge is perpendicular. The descriptors which archaeologically differentiate the two classes of wood-working tools are the symmetricity of the edge and the traces of work. Thus, at the beginning of the second iteration there is the following descriptive system: length, width, thickness, presence of edge, symmetricity of the edge, presence of characteristic traces of work. The synthesis of structures based on this descriptive system and the following interpretation may differentiate between the axes and the adzes.

(3) The axes, taken separately, can be expected to be either tools or weapons (or symbols). This leads to the addition of descriptors such as the softness of the stone material, the weight, the sex and age of the deceased with whom an axe is found in a grave, the position of axes in graves in relation to the body, etc. This may possibly lead to the recognition of weapons. Further iterations may discover chronological variations.

Thus, archaeological knowledge, like any other kind of knowledge, is never complete: when progress is made in the field of theory, all relevant evidence should be 'reworked' by means of the archaeological method. Whenever new finds are made, theories must be reconsidered in the light of such new data, once more using the archaeological method.

There are two assumptions which tend to obscure the process of obtaining new knowledge. According to one of them, any discipline develops in a catastrophic way: a new step is not a continuation of the preceding one, being rather its complete negation. Analysis of how archaeology actually developed in the past disclosed that the catastrophic change did not apply. Any new paradigm, and any new iteration as described in the preceding paragraphs, was deeply rooted in the previous states of archaeology. The increment of new knowledge achieved in a single step or iteration is usually slight.

The other assumption is that the role of the individual archaeologist is so important that he or she can never arrive at an objective reconstruction of the past. There is no doubt that any archaeological writing is conditioned by its author. However, to claim absolute subjectivity on this basis is at least as questionable as to claim absolute objectivity.

The iterative way to the past is rarely simple or linear but, on the whole, it brings us nearer to the approximation of human history.

Bibliography

Binford, L. R. 1962 Archaeology as anthropology, *American Antiquity* 28, 217–25.
1964 A consideration of archaeological research design, *American Antiquity* 29, 425–41.
1968 Archaeological perspectives. In S. R. Binford and L. R. Binford (eds.), *New Perspectives in Archaeology*, pp. 5–32. Chicago: Aldine.
1972 *An Archaeological Perspective*. New York: Seminar Press.
Binford, L. R. and S. R. Binford 1966 A preliminary analysis of functional variability in the Mousterian of Levallois facies, *American Anthropologist* 68, 238–95.
Bujna, J. 1982 Spiegelung der Sozialstruktur auf latènezeitlichen Gräberfeldern im Karpatenbecken, *Památky Archaeologické* 73, 312–431.
Chang, K. C. 1967 *Rethinking Archaeology*. New York: Random House.
Childe, V. G. 1956 *Piecing Together the Past*. London: Routledge and Kegan Paul.
Clarke, D. L. 1968 *Analytical Archaeology*. London: Methuen.
Deetz, J. 1967 *Invitation to Archaeology*. New York: The Natural History Press.
de Saussure, F. 1974 *Course in General Linguistics*. Fontana.
Doran, J. E. and F. R. Hodson 1975 *Mathematics and Computers in Archaeology*. Edinburgh: Edinburgh University Press.
Eggers, H. J. 1959 *Einführung in die Vorgeschichte*. Munich: Piper and Co.
Eggert, M. K. H. 1978 Prähistorische Archäologie und Ethnologie: Studien zur amerikanischen New Archaeology, *Praehistorische Zeitschrift* 53(1), 6–146.
Gardin, A. 1979 *Une Archéologie théorique*. Paris: Hachette.
Gening, V. F. 1983 *Ob'yekt i predmet nauki v arkheologii*. Kiev: Naukova dumka.
Gould, R. A. and M. B. Schiffer 1981 *Modern Material Culture: The Archaeology of Us*. New York and London: Academic Press.

Harman, H. H. 1967 *Modern Factor Analysis*. Chicago: The University of Chicago Press.

Hensel, W. 1986 Archaeologia. Treść i zakres – Archaeology. Substance and range. In Hensel, Donato and Tabaczyński 1986, pp. 17–28.

Hensel, W., G. Donato and S. Tabaczyński 1986 *Teoria i praktyka badań archeologicznych*, Tom 1 – *Theory and Practice of Archaeological Research*. Vol. 1. Warsaw: Ossolineum.

Hodder, I. 1982 *Symbols in Action*. Cambridge: Cambridge University Press.

1986 *Reading the Past*. Cambridge: Cambridge University Press.

Kleyn, L. S. 1978 *Arkheologicheskie istochniki*. Leningrad: Izd. Leningradskogo universiteta.

Kuhn, T. 1962 *The Structure of Scientific Revolutions*. Chicago: The University of Chicago Press.

Malmer, M. 1962 *Jungneolithische Studien*. Lund: H. Ohlssons.

Megaw, J. V. S. 1984 The archaeology of rubbish or rubbishing archaeology: backward looks and forward glances, *Australian Historical Archaeology* 2, 7–12.

Montelius, O. 1903 *Die älteren Kulturperioden im Orient und in Europa I. Die Methode*. Stockholm: Selbstverlag.

Neustupný, E. 1958 Evolution in archaeology. In *Epitymbion Roman Haken*, pp. 4–8. Prague: Societas Archaeologica Bohemoslovenica.

1964 Společnost kultury kulovitých amfor ve středoevropském eneolitu. Most 1964: MS of thesis.

1967 K počátkům patriarchátu ve střední Evropě – The beginnings of patriarchy in Central Europe (Rozpravy ČSAV 77/2). Prague: Academia.

1968 Absolute chronology of the Neolithic and Eneolithic periods in Central and South-Eastern Europe, *Slovenská Archaeológia* 16, 19–60.

1969 Absolute chronology of the Neolithic and Eneolithic periods in Central and South-East Europe II, *Archeologické Rozhledy* 21, 783–810.

1971 Whither archaeology?, *Antiquity* 45, 34–9.

1973a Factors determining the variability of the Corded Ware culture. In C. Renfrew (ed.), *The Explanation of Culture Change*, pp. 725–30. London: Duckworth.

1973b Jednoduchá metoda archeologické analýzy – A simple method of archaeological analysis, *Památky Archeologické* 64, 169–234.

1976 Paradigm Lost. In *Glockenbechersymposium Oberried 1974*, pp. 241–8. Bussum-Haarlem: Fibula.

1978 Mathematics at Jenišův Újezd. In J. Waldhauser (ed.), *Das keltische Gräberfeld bei Jenišův Újezd in Böhmen II*, pp. 40–66. Teplice: Krajské muzeum.

1983 The demography of prehistoric cemeteries, *Památky Archaeologické* 74, 7–34.

1986 Nástin archaeologické metody – An outline of the archeological method, *Archeologické Rozhledy* 38, 515–39.

1991 Recent theoretical achievements in prehistoric archaeology in Czechoslovakia. In Ian Hodder (ed.), *Archaeological Theory in Europe: The Last Three Decades*, pp. 248–71. London: Routledge.

Neustupný, J. V. 1958 Prehistory and linguistics. In *Epitymbion Roman Haken*, pp. 12–14. Prague: Societas Archaeologica Bohemoslovenica.

1978 *Post-Structural Approaches to Language*. Tokyo: University of Tokyo Press.

Pałubicka, A. and S. Tabaczyński 1986 Społeczeństwo i kultura jako przedmiot badań archeologicznych – Society and culture as object of archeological studies. In Hensel, Donato and Tabaczyński 1986, pp. 57–183.

Plog, F. and D. L. Carlson, 1989 Computer applications for the All American Pipeline Project, *Antiquity* 63, 258–67.

Renfrew, C. 1969 The autonomy of the east European Copper Age, *Proceedings of the Prehistoric Society* 35, 12–47.

1987 *Archaeology and Language*. London: Jonathan Cape.

Renfrew, C. and G. Sterud 1969 Close-proximity analysis: a rapid method for the ordering of archaeological materials, *American Antiquity* 34(3), 265–77.

Schiffer, M. B. 1972 Archaeological context and systemic context, *American Antiquity* 37, 156–65.

1976 *Behavioural Archaeology*. New York: Academic Press.

Shennan, S. 1976 Bell Beakers and their context in Central Europe. In *Glockenbechersymposium Oberried 1974*, pp. 231–9. Bussum-Haarlem: Fibula.

1988. *Quantifying Archaeology*. Edinburgh: Edinburgh University Press.

Sokal, R. S. and F. J. Rohlf 1981 *Biometry* (2nd edition). New York: Freeman and Co.

Spaulding, A. C. 1960 The dimensions of archaeology. In J. E. Dole and R. L. Carneiro (eds.), *Essays in the Science of Culture: In Honor of Leslie A. White*, pp. 437–56.

Urbańczyk, P. 1986 Formowanie się układów stratyfikacyjnych jak proces źródłotwórczy – The formation of stratificational entities as a source-creative process. In Hensel, Donato and Tabaczyński 1986, pp. 184–245.

Waldhauser, J. (ed.) 1978 *Das keltische Gräberfeld bei Jenišův Újezd in Böhmen*, 2 vols. Teplice: Krajské muzeum.

Index

For EU product safety concerns, contact us at Calle de José Abascal, 56–1°,
28003 Madrid, Spain or eugpsr@cambridge.org.

www.ingramcontent.com/pod-product-compliance
Ingram Content Group UK Ltd.
Pitfield, Milton Keynes, MK11 3LW, UK
UKHW012345130625
459647UK00009B/541